PASTOR'S HANDBOOK
VOL. I

CHRISTIAN CARE BOOKS
Wayne E. Oates, Editor

PASTOR'S HANDBOOK

Vol. I

by

Wayne E. Oates

THE WESTMINSTER PRESS
Philadelphia

Book Design by Dorothy Alden Smith

Published by The Westminster Press®
Philadelphia, Pennsylvania

PRINTED IN THE UNITED STATES OF AMERICA
9 8 7 6 5 4 3

Library of Congress Cataloging in Publication Data

Oates, Wayne Edward, 1917–
    Pastor's handbook.

    Ministerial supplement to the first six
vols. of Christian care books.
    Includes bibliographies.
    1. Pastoral theology—Handbooks, manuals, etc.
    2. Pastoral psychology—Handbooks, manuals,
etc. I. Title. II. Christian care books.
BV4016.0'17   253   79–28639
ISBN 0–664–24300–2

To
Altus Newell, Ph.D.
My Pastor

Contents

Acknowledgments

I am primarily indebted to my secretary, Mrs. Jenni Khaliel, for the highly professional care she has given to this book. She developed a fund of technical data for my assessment as I wrote the book. She corrected my original manuscript and typed it with remarkable precision. Her efficiency has made the book possible.

I am also indebted to the authors of the first six Westminster Christian Care Books—William Arnold, George Bennett, Jan Cox-Gedmark, John Hewett, Wade and Mary Jo Rowatt, and Paul Schmidt—for their superb work, because I have had the advantage of reading their manuscripts before writing the corresponding chapters of this book. Their competence and dedication to their tasks facilitated my work.

I am grateful also to the late Harry Nickles for his professional skill in the final copy-editing of the manuscript.

I treasure the confidence placed in me by innumerable counselees and patients by whose suffering I have been taught. Through them and my effort in this volume, may pastors in great numbers become skilled in the care of many others.

W.E.O.

University Hospital—2H
323 E. Chestnut Street
Louisville, Kentucky

Introduction
Pastoral Use of Literature

LITERATURE AS AN INSTRUMENT
OF WISDOM AND CARE

This book is written to you as a pastor. You are my audience. The audience of a letter, a pamphlet, or a book shapes the message being written as surely as does the written word itself. Both the audience and the medium of expression are shaping influences on what is said, how it is said, and what the content means. An esteemed friend, Russell Dicks, who was the editor of the Westminster Pastoral Aid Series, said to me in 1949 about writing a book: "Remember, you can't go with each copy of your book to explain what you mean. You have to put what you mean in the words." That is what the authors of the Westminster Christian Care Books have done. They have not written directly to you as a pastor, but to your parishioner, your counselee, your member of the Christian life and growth group, and your congregation. You yourself or your friends may be going through some of the critical experiences described in the books. Each book is written as a tool for you as a pastor to use skillfully in your care of the afflicted. You may simply suggest the appropriate book, to be bought at the bookstore or borrowed from you. You may refer to the book in a sermon or in talking with a group you are leading. The contents have been tailored to your need for reliable literature as an aid for conveying wisdom and care to the persons whom you serve.

PURPOSES OF THIS BOOK

You may well ask: "If the Westminster Christian Care Books are so useful, why must I spend time reading what you are saying here?" You can benefit by reading this book because of the several reasons for which it is written:

First, I can converse directly with you *as the pastor* about how to use the Westminster Christian Care Books and other pertinent writings to the best advantage in your pastoral care of individuals. Your education, your wide contacts, and your responsibility as a leader of worship prompt people to look to you, not only as a private, one-to-one confidant but also as a teacher. A teacher needs written materials for homework on the issues of life which become critical from time to time.

If you do not perceive this need now, think back through the last six months or so. Recount the number of times someone has said to you: "Do you know of anything I could read about . . . ?" You have groped through your computerlike mind, but it does not print out a thing. One reason it doesn't print out anything is that some subjects have simply not been discussed in books. For example, we could not find any popular literature addressed directly to the families of persons who had committed suicide. Therefore we asked John Hewett to write on the needs of such families, so that now, even if you are not asked for help, you have fresh new options in this and the other books of the series. You, pastoral colleague, have seen more than the one experience such persons present. However, all persons may be strengthened by you and the Holy Spirit if they can read about a broad spectrum of others who are going through similar experiences. Moreover, these books make available, in plain English, the thinking of behavioral scientists about such experiences and human reactions to them.

A second purpose prompts this book. You as a minister need more than a popular book can offer on the subjects of these first six Westminster Christian Care volumes. The content of this book you are now reading aims at providing you with more technical background on these subjects and suggests how you may continually update your knowledge of them. The world of today is like a swift, white-spumed river. As the ancients said, you can't put your foot in the same river twice, because it flows too fast. Today you and I struggle to negotiate the rapids. We are not interested in merely putting our foot in the same river; we want to move steadily with the current. But it is not easy to keep up with the concerns of our people, and it is even harder to keep ahead of them. Yet that is part of your prophetic task and mine. When we do so, we can both comfort our people wisely and protect them by observing early signs of trouble. Thus, one purpose of this volume is to enable you to stay several steps ahead of your people. And in the process of enabling you, I equip myself at the same time.

A third reason for this book is the desirability of prevention. What can we learn from the experience of a family rearing a child that has Down's syndrome? How can we help other families to avoid this problem? Jan Cox-Gedmark, in her Westminster Christian Care Book, speaks eloquently of a variety of situations that give people "no end" grief—a kind of grief that differs from that induced by someone's death, which is only one of several kinds of grief. Some, though not all, instances of chronic grief can be avoided, and one of the purposes of the following chapters is to suggest a few means of prevention. Thus, you as a pastor may take part in that primary, front-line effort at preventing certain difficulties that often escalate and accumulate to such an extent that people trying to cope with them end up in the hospital. Hospitalization is too often a last stand against overwhelming odds. Much can and needs to be learned from detailed analysis of the long history of persons whose health has collapsed under emotional burdens. That knowledge is best used at the earliest appearance of the possibility of any problem. You are often—certainly not always—in touch with people at those moments in their lives when a little attention and wisely used information can do the most good to forestall unnecessary suffering. (See Gerald Caplan's *Principles of Preventive Psychiatry;* Basic Books, 1964.)

A fourth purpose of this book is to confer with you on the art of using literature as an instrument in your pastoral wisdom and care. In particular, the careful and artistic use of the Westminster Christian Care Books is worth some separate and concentrated attention. The rest of this introduction is devoted to that subject. The succeeding chapters will give you professional background and predictive help in preventing unnecessary suffering insofar as is possible, as well as background material of value to you as a pastor.

THE ART OF USING LITERATURE IN PASTORAL CARE

Literature is an assistant and not a substitute for you

In my work I need all the shortcuts I can find. Don't you? The importance of conserving time and energy increases; it never diminishes. As it increases, you and I are faced ethically with the choice between legitimate ways of saving time and energy and those illegitimate ones that are wrong and leave us with feelings of anxious, defensive guilt. These guilts accumulate from day to day and make us feel unclean. Paradoxically, we become busier and busier with more and more superficial tasks.

One shortcut neither you nor I can afford to take is to substitute a book for a personal relationship. God, in the fullness of time, decided that no book would effect your redemption and mine. Therefore, he sent Jesus Christ in person, in the flesh, the Word made flesh. The people of his day could see, hear, touch, and sense his compassion, anger, companionship, and power to set us free from bondage. The best of literature concentrates the truth and wisdom that must come alive in the spirit of a caring person. You and I are presumptuous to assume that we are ambassadors for Christ and continue in the church the body of Christ. But we must be sure of our relationship to Christ. Through the corporate personhood of the church and its ministry, the love of God and neighbor is extended to all people, whether in distress or in celebration. No written word can substitute for this personal relationship. Literature is like a road map; it directs and points. It is not the road itself. It can aid you as an interpreter; it cannot take your place; it is no substitute for *you*. This is why we call these volumes the Westminster Christian Care Books. They are intended to complement, assist, and aid—not to replace—your care of persons.

Furthermore, these books can evoke negative reactions in your counselees as well as positive suggestions that they embrace as their own. The author is not present. Both you and the counselees can freely disagree with him or her. It is hoped that these books and others like them will facilitate and even shorten your task as a pastoral counselor by bringing negative feelings to the surface and exposing blockages to growth.

Choose a book that speaks directly and personally to the person who has a certain problem

I have chosen in this book to talk directly and personally to you as a fellow Christian pastor. Your parish probably is in the context of a congregation. Mine happens to be in the context of a school of medicine where I am expected to be a pastor and a teacher. Our situations differ, but they have much in common. I serve as a consultant in pastoral care on the staff of the St. Matthews Baptist Church. Weekly I am in touch with the kinds of situations that you as a parish clergyperson encounter. Consequently, I can speak with you personally and directly. This is not a third-person textbook. It is a personal communication to you as a pastor, not a book that you would necessarily hand to a parishioner. It is addressed directly and personally to you. If your parishioners do read it, it may help them to understand you and your work better. This in itself is an advantage. Maybe your official board members would benefit too. Often they have no clear notion of what your invisible responsibilities as a pastor are. However, the family with a member who suffers a real character disorder, who is often in trouble with the law, and who is beyond their control do not need this book. Instead, they need Paul Schmidt's book on character disorders and how one member of a family can and does cause inordinate trouble. Schmidt's book is addressed directly and personally to such a family with such a member in mind.

You will choose other pastoral-aid books besides these six. There is an elaborate paperback publication list with a wealth of books that are fairly inexpensive and easy to carry. Therefore, an important criterion for choosing a book is: "Is it addressed directly and personally to those who are hurting?"

Are those to whom you are handing a book able to read? If so, do they like to read and do they actually read?
Literacy in the parishioner is one of the assumptions of the pastoral use of literature as an instrument of wisdom and care. Some people have never learned to read. Even persons with college and postgraduate educations may not like to read, perhaps because they associate reading with taking and pass-

ing tests. Hence, they may perceive you as a teacher who is going to quiz them on the contents—an attitude you do not want! So it is best carefully to assess whether a parishioner in need of help can benefit from reading.

One special person you will encounter is the one who has poor or failing eyesight or who is blind. Anyone totally sightless may use Braille or the excellent resources of cassette tapes. Then, too, you can use part of an interview to read to such persons carefully selected passages, especially from the Bible. You can inquire among persons close to them to learn who would have time to read to them. Members of your congregation could be enlisted to perform the same task.

Furthermore, even if you discover one or several persons in your congregation who cannot read even though they have good eyesight, you have found an additional outlet for ministry. The church is an educational institution that is completely voluntary, does not award degrees, does not often give examinations even on a pass-fail system. In this aspect of its work, the church is preeminently a "school without failure."

You may not have illiterate people in your congregation. However, if you ask how many of those able to read actually spend time reading, or enjoy reading, you would find numerous "illiterates." Yet we expect such persons to "read" their Bibles! A consistent and sustained encouragement of reading enriches the lives of your parishioners; it opens old and creates new channels of reception of the good news of Jesus Christ. Later in this introduction I will offer specific suggestions on how you may encourage your congregation to read more. My point here is that you and I should find out whether people care and desire to read when we contemplate handing them a book about one or more of their personal problems.

A fourth principle to observe in giving out any kind of literature is timing. If someone asks for a certain book with no prompting from you, there is no problem of timing. That is a perfect instance of a "teachable moment." It is all the more important, then, for you to offer just the right suggestion—the fitting book for the particular moment. Moreover, the request permits you actually to open a serious conversation with someone whose relationship to you has been only superficial. The book may focus and push to a deeper level your dialogue with the person, couple, or family. In fact, some persons will initiate a pastoral counseling relationship with you by saying: "I have been reading this book, and would like to talk with you about it." If you watch Billy Graham, Oral Roberts, the PTL Club, the Seven Hundred Club, and other such programs on television, you will note them recommending, giving, or selling literature to their audiences. The recipients may be your parishioners, who will read it and perhaps ask you what you think of it. You would be happier, I assume, if you yourself had made the original suggestion from the pulpit or in a more informal group. If a book is available and recommended, however, by you or by others, people tend to ask you as their pastor what you think of it, and this provides another "teachable moment."

If you are holding a series of counseling interviews with an individual, then timing is of the essence in lending or recommending a book. As Carroll Wright, director of the Los Angeles City Mission Society's Pastoral Counseling Center, says, requesting a book may be a shy person's way of asking you to show concern. If you sense that this may be true, you could ask: "Is this something you will read for personal reasons or for a friend? In either case I would be glad, and have the time, to talk with you about your interest and to consider which other books would be most helpful." For example, if persons whose parents have been recently divorced ask you for a book on divorce, you can surmise they want to think systematically about what has happened. You can recommend William Arnold's book in the Westminster Christian Care

Books series and offer to sit down with them at their convenience and discuss the book and how it impresses them, thus inviting useful dialogue.

A fifth principle of the pastoral use of literature is to consider not only the individual but the individual's family. The book by Arnold on divorce can be handed to an eighteen- or twenty-year-old person who is still living at home with one or the other parent. If the young person takes the book home and lays it on a table, the chances are strong that the parent will also read it. Do you want this to happen? In many instances, the book would be helpful to both the parent and the grown son or daughter. If, however, there is conflict between the generations, the book itself can be another source of conflict. Even so, you may decide on the basis of your knowledge of both sides that the book might catalyze a more creative conflict and encourage both to face the deeper issues more humbly. Your decision and assessment, not some outsider's, must be followed. You decide what is in the best interests of the whole family of the individual.

A final principle of the pastoral use of literature is the degree of spiritual support and accurate empathy the author reflects to the reader. To assess a book on this principle, you yourself must have read either the book or a careful review of it by someone whose judgment you respect. You need not have read line for line every book you recommend. However, candor is of the essence at such times:

"I frankly have not read this book. I have only learned about it. If you should read it before I do, would you give me your opinion of it? This will help me to help other people, too."

or,

"I have read the table of contents, the chapter outline, and the bibliography the author uses. It appears to be a good book, but I have not read it closely."

or,

"As you may know, I, too, have had a close relative who was hospitalized for psychiatric illnesses. George Bennett's book on the convalescence of mental patients made real sense to me. It helped me to think through and reshape my whole approach to my relative. I read the book line for line and would be glad to share my copy with you."

These three responses reflect differing degrees of strength of recommendation. In each, the forthright candor commends the book at a different level.

LITERATURE AND THE ENRICHMENT OF THE LIFE OF THE CHURCH

You as a pastor work in the dynamic field of relationships in your church congregation. The corporate life of the congregation can be guided, enriched, and ennobled when your parishioners are encouraged to read books together as neighbors, as small-group members in Sunday school classes, growth groups, and study groups, and as they worship together under the tutelage of your preaching. Several suggestions are in order for the function and place of literature in the life of your congregation as a whole. I do not see the pastoral use of literature as being an aid only to your work as a counselor of individuals in private, one-to-one relationships. Rather, the use of literature as a source of pastoral wisdom and care concerns equally your administrative, teaching, organizing, and outreach functions. In the rest of the introduction I shall make some specific suggestions.

First, your sermons themselves can become "homemade" literature for your congregation if you use a copying machine to reproduce each Sunday's sermon, to be made available on the following Sunday. In addition to providing your people with literature for their own use, a few of them may say: "I took a second copy to give to my friend at work. He's going through some problems and I think your sermon will give him some real hope." Some will keep a file of sermons, others will carry certain ones in their pockets, or purses, and many will discuss them at home. They have a word-for-word account of what you said in case they misunderstood you. It may be the basis for a small-group discussion or a personal conference. Some of the most effective preachers I have heard make a practice of providing copies of their sermons to their congregations.

The topics of the first six Westminster Christian Care Books in and of themselves call for some attention from the pulpit. A sermon on the *abilities* of the handicapped could draw heavily on the insights in Jan Cox-Gedmark's book on chronic sorrow. A sermon on being "wise as serpents and innocent as doves" (Matt. 10.16) could capture the importance of the "tough loving care" suggested by Paul Schmidt for dealing with character-disordered people. A sermon on creative alternatives to futility could carefully concentrate on the importance of talking about the temptation to suicide and the equal importance of taking people seriously who do talk about committing suicide. John Hewett's book will be primary source material for preparing such a sermon. The care of the sick in the home is an emerging response to the high cost of hospitalization today. Jesus lived in a time when this was the rule and not the exception. The care of the convalescing mentally ill person can be discussed as openly as one would discuss Jesus' ministry to Peter's mother-in-law (Matt. 8:14–15). The critical issues of working parents, the importance of self-reliance in growing children, and the possibilities of work as a strengthening factor in the home are dealt with by Wade and Mary Jo Rowatt. You could devise a sermon around the "Establishment of the Works of Our Hands" referred to in Ps. 90:16–17. ("Let thy work be manifest to thy servants, and thy glorious power to their children. Let the favor of the Lord our God be upon us, and establish thou the work of our hands upon us, yea, the work of our hands establish thou it.") Such sermons could be occasional or parts of a series on life situations. When reinforced by the distribution of copies of each sermon, its effects will be multiplied.

In the second place, the church itself can develop and emphasize a library as a means of spiritual growth. This library could circulate pastoral-aid books selected by you. Libraries require money, but the funds can be budgeted. You as a pastor can promote the use of the library by regularly requisitioning books to be ordered and paid for by the church. You can ask the publishers of religious books to put you on their mailing lists, and from their catalogs you can select the books to be ordered for the church as a routine exercise of your leadership.

A books-for-sale program can greatly enrich the life of your people. I recall living in New York for two years, during which I attended Riverside Church. It was a real pleasure to browse through its bookstore before or after services. I am sure the store made considerable income, because it was crowded. Similarly, a bookstore in your locality could work with your official board to establish an extension or branch to serve your people. Or you could arrange occasional special book sales in connection with family-life emphasis programs, intensive Bible-study weeks, and other such activities. Or, if you wanted to limit your bookselling, you could pick certain books or series of books and give them special attention as they are published. I could hope that you will make at least such a trial run with the Westminster Christian Care Books.

You as a pastor of today are in a simple, elementary form of ministry if you depend solely upon direct face-to-face conversation. Of course, there is no substitute for the personal relationship, but when you use literature, it acts like another medium for the growth of that relationship in trust, wisdom, and care. When you use literature to enhance your ministry, you multiply your outreach and intensify your personal and pastoral influence. When you introduce another person's book to your parishioner, you are calling on the author as a consultant, for a second opinion. New approaches are suggested, and those you have used are reinforced or modified. The community of learning has been enlarged. We, the authors of the Westminster Christian Care Books, pray that this community of learning, embracing you, your parishioners, and us, will be led by the Holy Spirit, the great counselor given to us by God upon the request of our Lord Jesus Christ.

1. Divorce Between Parents of Adult Sons and Daughters

The aftermath of divorce in the lives of adult sons and daughters of divorcees is no secret to you as a pastor. You may share the feelings of the pastor who described the following situations:

1. A twenty-six-year-old woman calls you and asks you to perform her wedding ceremony. You have known her most of her life as a friend of the family. You are deeply committed to fostering her happiness. You as her pastor have stood with her at milestones such as high-school commencement, choosing a college, graduation from college, an illness from which she suffered and recovered. Such bonds are strong. You agree to perform the ceremony. Yet you know that her parents were recently divorced, and that both of them have remarried. Which parent is going to attend the daughter's wedding? You are concerned because she spent most of the first discussion of her wedding talking about her parents' divorce and remarriages.

2. A seventeen-year-old college freshman, a super high achiever—a "brain"—calls you. He is upset. He has been given a hard time by his buddies in the freshman class. They think he is an "egghead," a "gung ho grade-getting idiot," somebody who does not seek pleasure. They make fun of him for his scholastic superiority and his awkwardness with

women. He says: "I thought I would call you. I knew you would understand." "Well," you say, "how are things with you?" "I just don't like myself very much," he says. You know that just before he finished high school, his mother coldly rejected his somewhat inadequate father and the two of them were divorced. He seldom sees his mother because she lives in a distant state and has remarried. His father, though wealthy, rides his back all the time, making fun of his academic interests, too.

3. An eighteen-year-old young man calls you at Christmastime. He is home for the holidays after his first semester in college. He too is upset. He had counted on his father to pay the tuition for his second semester, but his parents were divorced three months ago. His father, he says, told him: "I can't help you. Get your mother to help you. She has all my money. Or get out and work for it yourself, as I had to when I was your age."

You search the literature on divorce and its effects on sons and daughters who are adults. You find a modest amount of reading material about the impact of divorce on small children. You read Richard A. Gardner's book, *The Boys and Girls Book About Divorce* (Bantam Books, 1971), and move on to his more technical book, *Psychotherapy with Children of Divorce* (Jason Aronson, 1976). The critical question of when and how to tell a small child about impending divorce, such legal problems as custody and visitation privileges, are discussed in these valuable books. You read them with faithful attention because the Holy Spirit brings back to your memory what Jesus taught about small children (Matt. 18:1–11).

Yet all of this is background preparation for the pastoral situations in which you search for a book addressed to *adult* sons and daughters whose parents divorce. The young people described in the three case situations above are all over sixteen years of age. Maybe their parents stayed together a few years "for the children's sake," and as soon as their children were old enough to take care of themselves—whether they had learned to do so or not—decide to get a divorce. Now the divorce is an accomplished fact with which the adult son or daughter—often married and raising children—must deal in one way or another. If you search for literature on this problem, the best volume among the few you will find is William Arnold's book in the Westminster Christian Care Books series. He has tailored his text to be read by the sons or daughters and by their parents or grandparents. This chapter in this book is a companion essay to speak with you as a pastor about your care of the older sons and daughters of divorced persons.

The Frequency of Divorce in Middle and Later Maturity

How often does divorce occur among parents whose sons and daughters are sixteen and older? (I choose sixteen because in many states this is the age at which a person is no longer legally required to attend public school, can go to work without parental or legal permission or restraint, and—with parental consent—can legally drive an automobile.) If the parents were married at the age of eighteen and their oldest child is sixteen, then the couple would be about thirty-five at the time of their divorce, though often they will be much older. The 1978 vital statistics report on an age-differentiated frequency of divorce is revealing.

In 1977, there were 10.1 marriages and 5 divorces per 1,000 population. "This marked the first time since 1966 that there has not been an increase in the annual divorce rate." (*Vital Statistics Report*, Vol. 26, No. 13, December 7, 1978, p. 13; Department of Health, Education, and Welfare, Publication No. (PHS) 79-1120.) The *1977 Statistical Abstract* gives 1976 data on the rate of divorces as

5 per 1,000 population. These are divorces that were obtained during the year 1976. (*Statistical Abstract, 1977,* p. 55; U.S. Department of Commerce, Bureau of the Census, 1977.) This figure of 5 per 1,000 represents frequency of divorces granted in that year. When we consult the same issue of the *Statistical Abstract* for the percentage of persons 25 to 54 years old who had ever been married and who were divorced, we find figures of 5.8 percent for men and 8.4 percent for women. In age-sex groups they were:

MALES	FEMALES
25–34—6.0%	25–34—8.8%
35–44—5.8%	35–44—9.0%
45–54—5.5%	45–54—7.4%

(Statistical Abstract, p. 75.)

In an age-sex differentiation covering a longer time span, showing the differences between the general census of 1960 and that of 1970, the "characteristics of the population" as a whole become apparent in the table below. In both men and women, the increase of rate of divorce starts at the thirty to thirty-four age group, peaks with those to fifty to fifty-four, begins to decline with the sixty to sixty-four age group, but does not equal the twenty to twenty-four group until people live to be eighty to eighty-four.

The highest rates in the table above are for women, indicating a higher rate of remarriage for men in each age group, and for women, a higher need for personal survival skills as divorced persons not yet remarried. All the rates in the table below show women to be at much greater financial risk for having to live alone and draw on family, community, church, and state support than are men. In spite of the upsurge of liberation efforts by and for women, they are at least 30 percent more at a disadvantage than men in having to fend for themselves. This is true from the age group of fifteen to nineteen all the way up to that of seventy-five to seventy-nine, when the situation of men as a population and women as a population becomes the same.

By Age	1960 (p. 644) (DIVORCED)		1970 (pp. 640–41) (DIVORCED)	
	Males*	Females*	Males*	Females*
14	—	—	.1	.1
15–19	.1	.3	.1	.3
20–24	1.0	1.8	1.4	2.5
25–29	1.8	2.6	3.0	4.3
30–34	2.2	3.1	3.3	5.0
35–39	2.5	3.6	3.4	5.3
40–44	2.7	4.0	3.8	5.6
45–49	3.0	4.3	3.8	5.5
50–54	3.1	4.2	3.9	5.5
55–59	3.1	3.9	3.9	5.2
60–64	3.0	3.3	3.6	4.8
65–69	2.7	2.7	3.5	4.1
70–74	2.4	2.1	3.1	3.3
75–79	2.1	1.5	2.7	2.7
80–84	1.7	1.1	2.4	2.1
85+	1.4	.8	2.4	1.7

*% total of population.
(Characteristics of the Population, Vol. 1; Part 1, U.S. Summary, Section 2; U.S. Department of Commerce, Social and Economic Statistics Administration, Bureau of the Census.)

These population perspectives suggest several emphasis strategies for you and your church. What specifically can be done both to prevent and to ameliorate the impact of divorce upon everyone concerned?

First, when persons—both male and female—are between the ages of fourteen and twenty-four, they should be involved in programs that teach them economic and social survival

skills, not just how to perpetuate the fantasy life of cooperative play—a skill learned much earlier, between three and
thirteen—because to perpetuate the love of play, overdevelop
it, glorify it, and institutionalize it into anyone's concept of
adult sexuality in dating and courtship is to sow and reap a
whirlwind of marital unhappiness and high-risk existence in
the event of divorce.

Churches expend heavy budgets on youth and its activities,
recreation, play, and fun. The phrase "doing something for
the young people" connotes recreation. Little is done in high
schools and colleges to develop work-study-learning relationships. Yet the healthiest marriages tend to arise out of courtship situations that center on work and economic survival.
The aphorism "Courtship revolves around play; marriage revolves around work" needs challenging. My hypothesis is that
if churches can include vocational education in their approach to young persons, they will find a whole new pro-
phylaxis against the destruction of marriage known as divorce.
And if parents can be persuaded to cooperate, they will be less
likely to be overburdened by "lazy"—their word—adolescents who use the family home for summer sexual escapades
while their elders are at work. When they meet in work
situations, they don't need baby-sitters at the age of fifteen
or eighteen!

Careful study of religious groups that have traditionally
practiced the disciplines of teaching their youth to work and
to survive confirms my point of view. You will find it revealing
to read Joseph W. Eaton's and Robert J. Weil's study of the
Hutterites of the Dakotas and southern Saskatchewan. (*Culture and Mental Disorders;* Free Press, 1955. Also by Eaton,
"Adolescence in a Communal Society," *Mental Hygiene,*
Vol. 48, No. 1, January 1964, pp. 66–73.) The old, tired
strategies simply intensify the tragedies of helpless adolescents who can't pay their freshman-year tuition because of

their parents' divorce. Devising new strategies is the pressing order of the day.

The reasons I emphasize survival-skill training as a preventive measure are threefold:

First, it seems to me that the modern family begins to rip and tear apart when the children are no longer small, when they become more of an economic demand, and when both mother and father feel exhausted from trying to control them. They are literally beyond anyone's control except their own and that of the police, in that order. Many of them are "consenting adults" above the age of eighteen and "on their own" in their thinking and fantasies, though very dependent economically. Many others, sixteen or older, are geographically beyond control through their use of automobiles. The quarrels over control of biologically mature but sociologically infantile sons and daughters are—from my clinical observation—a major contributing factor to husband-wife conflict that can spread out to involve social and job problems, and all conspire to set the stage for divorce if not to cause it.

Second, the actual demands laid upon you and me as pastoral counselors confirm my views to some convincing degree. For example, the partner in a divorce who has custody of the children tends to reach out to you and me as pastors for help in intense crises with the children. (The age of these "children" can range from six or seven to thirty!) The church and its ministers are sought out to fill part of the void both in the divorced person's and the children's lives. We of the church then go into action—when at our best—arranging summer-job interviews, getting in touch with job-training opportunities for divorced women, encouraging grants-in-aid for college students' support, conferring with young parents about how to handle visiting rights of a divorced parent who introduces their child to a second spouse who has recently replaced the child's grandmother or grandfather. If this is confusing, that is what such situations are like! No wonder you automatically ask, when you hear of a divorce between unknown persons in their forties, fifties, and sixties: "Do they have any sons and daughters?"

A third extrapolation from the age-focused statistics is that blaming marital disruption on "young people" is a cultural habit, an easy projection unsupported by the facts. The thirty to thirty-four age range introduces the national norm, not younger persons, and those forty and above stand at the peak. You as a pastor have, then, not only the care of the divorced couple but also the responsibility of being a consistent, steady person and introducing other such persons to the middle, late, and delayed adolescent sons and daughters of such marital break-ups and divorces.

THE REALIGNMENT OF YOUR PASTORAL RELATIONSHIPS

The event of divorce causes relatives and close friends to take sides. Your pastoral relationship is shaped by the inter-relatedness of these persons to the church family of which you are a part. In any event your pastoral relationship undergoes a change. It must be realigned. Several members of one family decided to return to church after the divorce of the parents. The five grown sons, the grandfather, and the mother appeared together. Yet they never came back a second time, because they heard the pastor make a negative side remark about the hardness of heart of persons who obtain divorces. Later, when he saw them at their place of business, they were cordial, formal, and cold. Another family sustains a very deep relationship to the church—mother, sons, daughters-in-law and grandchildren. But the father severed his relationship to pastor and church. Another family consisted of five grown sons with families of their own. After the divorce, the mother left the community, but the father, sons, daughters-in-law, and grandchildren continued to be active in the church. When the father remarried, however, one of the sons rejected his new stepmother and ceased to attend church. The pastor nevertheless realigned his relationship to the angry son by consistent pastoral visitation and attention to the man's whole family. The patience and wisdom required in these intricate realignments of a pastor's relationship are massive. Yet to identify the task as a routine procedure, one that is required of you, puts your mind to work lighting candles and not cursing the darkness.

INTERPRETING DIVORCE TO AN ADULT SON OR DAUGHTER

You are an interpreter of life's events to your counselees. They are more often than not so discouraged that they see only one possible interpretation of their parents' divorce. The "dark" interpretations they choose are one or more of these: "Were they thinking of this all along as we were growing up? If so, they sure did keep us fooled." "I was the youngest. As soon as I left home they got a divorce. Was I the cause of it? Was I the straw that broke the camel's back?" "We never had a home anyway. We just went through the motions. I guess it's just as well."

The Death of a Relationship

Your task and mine as pastors is to enable the troubled person to cast the events onto a larger screen for better understanding. One major interpretation of divorce is what some theologians today are calling "the death of a relationship." Joseph A. McAvoy is quoted by Richard McCormick, S.J., as asking: "If the church allows, for example, the remarriage of widows, is this not to admit that the marital project ceases when mutual presence is sundered by death? And if this is so, is it impossible to conceive of a sundering of mutual presence when love is irremediably dead, when there is a radical affective separation?" ("Divorce and Remarriage," *The Catholic Mind*, Vol. 73, November 1975, p. 43.) Real Biblical and theological problems are neatly bypassed by this interpretation, not the least of which is the imperative of teachableness of both partners and the Christian commitment to forgiveness as a way of life. However, a son or daughter can be encouraged to consider how a relationship of love can be killed by hardhearted unteachableness or self-righteous unforgiveness. These reactions spring up between mates and are known to them and God; they are not matters for the adult son or daughter or the pastor to adjudicate.

A "No End" Grief Situation?

A less academic and more universally human interpretation of the suffering an adult son or daughter is experiencing is to see it as a profound "no end" grief experience. By "no end" I mean a grief that will extend throughout life and come up again and again for review with the very people initially involved. At first the grief is new; the wound is fresh. However, it will be there from now on. Sons and daughters can work through the shock, the numbness, the fantasy, and the sense of depression to a hardheaded realism. They can rebuild life on the assumption that the divorce really occurred. However, a part of the realism is that their parents are important to them, that things will not be the same again. Another part of the realism means that special events—a wedding, a funeral, some holidays, and times of serious illness—will tend to bring the divorce to mind again and again.

The Need to Rescue?

The important interpretation to convey to grown sons and daughters, however, is that the present grief *is* grief, that it can be worked through, and the disjointedness of their lives can be knitted together in a longer and more creative design than before. *They* are not doomed by the situation of their parents. *They* are not foreordained to be like them unless they choose to be. Neither are their parents' ways of life necessarily hopeless ones, even though some sons and daughters may see their mission in life as rescuing their parents, brothers, and sisters. Now that the divorce is a fact, such offspring may be grieved because they failed as rescuers. Perhaps for the first time, they may have encountered something beyond their control, something that simply could not be controlled. Now that the divorce has occurred, the need to be all powerful in the situation reasserts itself, and they neglect their own work, family life, friends and associates while working feverishly at trying to mend, make right, undo, or offset the effects of the divorce on one or both parents.

Letting Loose, Letting Go, Letting Be

Grown children who engross themselves in the rescue of parents from the results of a divorce are in something of the situation of the person in Matt. 8:21–22: "Another of the disciples said to him, 'Lord, let me first go and bury my father.' But Jesus said to him, 'Follow me, and leave the dead to bury their own dead.' " In order to get on with life, these people must not spend their whole energies trying to bury the aftermath of a parental divorce. They have their own lives to live, missions to perform, and callings as Christians to fulfill. The claims of discipleship of our Lord Jesus Christ are greater than the claims of parents. The care of our own spouses and children takes precedence over preoccupation with solving our parents' problems for them. In their hearts, parents know this and will subtly or forcefully resist a son's or daughter's most well-meaning suggestions as efforts to control them.

Therefore, you as a pastor are in an excellent position as a teacher of the gospel to encourage a son or daughter of divorced parents to "turn loose" from them, let them go their way and let them be themselves. The children do not abandon them when this is done. To the contrary, they treat their parents like the adults they are and expect them to function as such.

The business of "letting loose, letting go, and letting be" has a stern note to it. It is *tough* loving care. It enables a parent to adapt more quickly to the divorce, painful though that may be. And it keeps sons and daughters, especially when they may be relating to their parent of the opposite sex, out of the trap of becoming a substitute husband or wife. Clinically, I have observed adult sons and daughters being pushed by a parent and their own sense of duty to provide the companionship, the attentiveness, and even the financial support that ordinarily comes from a spouse who has abandoned these responsibilities. The pastor is in a key position to caution people against this and to urge them to attend to their own life callings and commitments without undue absorption in the stresses affecting divorced parents.

As I conclude this section on interpretations available to you as a Christian pastor, you may be wondering how directive you should be in people's life situations. In seminary you may have been taught to be passive, to listen empathetically and not to be aggressive, to interpret forthrightly, and not to be directive. To get a clear-cut perception of the inner struggles of human beings, these are important disciplines to observe. However, after you have achieved a good grasp of the problem, I do not think you need to feel that you must set aside the responsibilities you have as a teacher of the gospel in order to create a pseudopermissive environment when the events of divorce are coercive and chaos-producing, and call for a clear word of guidance from you.

In a conversation with Carl Rogers, the renowned pioneer in client-centered therapy, he told me that the pastor has responsibilities that demand action. However, he added, the pastor should, in discharging these duties, keep in mind the need for an attitude of genuineness, for a clear perception of the counselee's internal responsiveness to suggestions, and for a sense of the quality of relationship existing between the pastor and the parishioner. You can be reality-oriented and direct with people without overriding their sense of choice or putting yourself in God's place.

SOME HAZARDS TO OBSERVE AND AVOID

The grown son or daughter of divorced parents can be seen as one who feels desolate. Jesus said: "I will not leave you desolate." The word "desolate" can be translated in a more specific sense as "orphans." It means to be fatherless, bereft, friendless. It connotes the opposite of communion, fellowship, and ecstasy.

In their state of desolation, these bereaved persons endow you, the pastor, with a new importance. In many if not most divorce situations one or the other parent withdraws from daily interacting relationships, and that creates a void. You as a pastor are drawn into the vacuum; you are called to purify and authenticate your own faith by caring for the desolate as is indicated in James 1:27. ("Religion that is pure and undefiled before God and the Father is this: to visit orphans and widows in their affliction, and to keep oneself unstained from the world.")

Yet some of the hazards of such a high calling are noted even in the same verse. Your own impulse to rescue, control, undo, and even function as the redeemer yourself can mislead you into becoming overinvolved or can frighten you sufficiently to cause you to stand aside, do nothing, and abdicate all responsibility. What a narrow ridge upon which both to walk and to balance yourself! The Spirit of God alone can enable you to do so. As Jesus said to his disciples concerning certain healing tasks: "This kind cannot be driven out by anything but prayer" (Mark 9:29).

To your prayers add wisdom. Jesus advises that we "be wise as serpents and innocent as doves" (Matt. 10:16). Wisdom indicates that the level of hysteria and panic surrounding any divorce situation is very high. The reaching out to you as a pastor often is as desperate as that of drowning persons. In their last throes of effort, you and the resources of religious faith are clutched at hysterically, in severe panic, and they can carry you under with the panic in such a "plank grabber" syndrome of behavior.

The wisdom of the serpents and the guileless innocence of doves are your combined need. Such wisdom and guileless-ness indicate several specific strategies. I give them here as one who "has been there" more times than I can count. Yet I give them to you as one who knows in part and prophesies in part.

First, don't panic yourself. An angry, almost hysterical hus-band calls you and wants to see you in the next fifteen min-utes. You know that it would take you a half hour to get to him. Therefore, let him come to you, if you can at all see him then. Advise him to calm himself as much as he can and to drive with special care because you want him to arrive safely.

A thirty-year-old woman calls and says that she is alarmed about her parents' recent divorce. She has kept her husband up until two or three in the morning talking out her feelings about her parents' situation. Should mother come to live with them? She has to call her mother tonight. Can she talk with you now? This is the first you have known of the problem. Can you spare enough time to continue this conversation? You have a committee meeting in progress, and you don't like to keep six people waiting while you talk on the telephone with one. Tell her she deserves undivided attention. Calm her with a steady voice as you make a plan. Take her number if you do not already have it and give her a specific time when you can call back. Then phone her after you have finished your meeting, consulted any records you have about her and her parents, and gathered any data to which you have a discreet and appropriate access. Between her initial call and your return call, both of you have gained better control and are less likely to be in a state of panic. You have a clearer perspective.

Second, study the situation carefully—how it developed, what your caller's resources and other commitments are, and how disabled physically and emotionally the divorced parent is. In such matters it is important to learn whether relocating parents will uproot them from a congenial company in their own age group. Do they need medical attention? Are they so disabled as to need continuing hospital care and nursing attention? How old is the parent and with what earning potential? Such a review of the situation has therapeutic value for the daughter or son as well as diagnostic value for you. Your inspection of this is a data-gathering task to increase your wisdom as you "put it together" to make sense. The data-gathering has a *revealing* value for the son or daughter. They begin to see that their parent was in a panic state, also, when they called them. Then "slow it down," do an "instant replay," examine each movement more closely. If you have accomplished this, you have already prevented people from taking action on the basis of a judgment impaired by hysterical panic.

Third, ask yourself to what extent you—intentionally or not—are being nudged into the position of replacing the husband or wife in the lives of a couple's sons and daughters. You can "pinch-hit" in an emergency by supplying parentlike attention and care, but you cannot fulfill the functions of the partner who has left the scene in a divorce. Men who are contemplating a divorce—and may in fact be already committed to a divorce and perhaps over-committed to a possible second wife—often go to a pastoral counselor just before moving out of the house finally. They will say to you: "I love my wife and don't want to hurt her and the children, but I can't live with them any longer." Presently you will be asked if you would be willing to counsel with the wife also. You agree. An appointment is arranged when you will talk with her. You honestly see yourself as moving with them toward a reconciliation. However, even before you get the chance to see the wife, the husband moves out, announces that he is in love with someone else, and departs without notifying you. The next you hear is from the distraught wife, or one or more of the sons or daughters, or one or more of the parents of the husband or wife. You are left, then, by the departing husband to act in his place.

The best way to avoid this predicament is to anticipate it as a hidden agenda and air it as a possible happening in the first interview. If this is the person's intention, he should have an opportunity to say so then. (Let us continue with the husband in this role, though obviously the wife could play it too.) In a very real way, a husband who is tired of his marriage and wants to ease his conscience by getting pastoral counseling for his spouse and children is asking you to be responsible for someone he has already decided to forsake. If he is—intentionally or not—in fact abandoning his family into your care, I think it is best to confront him with the ethical violations that this course may involve.

In professional, fee-charging consultations, the ethical question of who will pay for the counseling time is one way of defining the confrontation. In the parish, where you as a clergyperson do not charge fees, I rather think that the continuing support of the church is a way of defining the confrontation. Does this person who is leaving his family plan also to leave the church? Where does he plan to attend church from here on? What is to be his relationship to God in Christ now? In his plans for his late-adolescent sons or daughters, what provisions is he making for their continued spiritual as well as economic support?

My own feeling is that we as pastors, in our attempts to be all things to all persons for all seasons, tend to evade such confrontations. In doing so, we virtually make our own task impossible because we take responsibility off the shoulders of those whose it rightly is. If, even after a confrontation, the man persists in bailing out, like someone parachuting out of a plane in midair, then the people left behind need attention and care. What then?

You as pastor of a church are in a unique position, after a divorce, to correlate the efforts of all the church members who are socially connected with the family. Each person's esteemed and trusted friends can be noted and encouraged to stay near. If there are an unusual number of persons in the church who have been hurt in loss through divorce, you as pastor can form a highly private group who will provide concerted support, and study and pray together. The important point is that you yourself not seek to bear all this alone. If you do, you will, as Jethro told Moses, "wear yourselves out, for the thing is too heavy for you; you are not able to perform it alone" (Ex. 18:18). Instead, mobilize the resources of the whole caring community.

One of the best ways of getting ready to do this for many at a time is to form a study group of people who need help in responding as Christians to their divorced or divorcing parents. Use William Arnold's book, *When Your Parents Divorce*, as a stimulus for conversation. Aim at strengthening those whose parents are divorced and enabling them to be of comfort to others who are going through this grief. The purpose of such study is to demonstrate that even painful situations like this can be made to praise God, even as the apostle Paul said in II Corinthians 1:3–4: "Blessed be the God and Father of our Lord Jesus Christ, the Father of mercies and God of all comfort, who comforts us in all our affliction, so that we may be able to comfort those who are in any affliction, with the comfort with which we ourselves are comforted by God."

SUGGESTIONS FOR FURTHER READING

Appleton, Jane, and Appleton, William. *How Not to Split Up.* Doubleday & Co., 1978.

Arnold, William V., et al. *Divorce: Prevention or Survival.* Westminster Press, 1977. Paperback.

Bach, George R., and Wyden, Peter. *The Intimate Enemy.* Avon Books, 1970.

Bennett, George F. *When They Ask for Bread.* John Knox Press, 1978.

Curran, Charles E. "Divorce: Catholic Theory and Practice in the United States—Part One." *The American Ecclesiastical Review,* Vol. 168, No. 1 (January 1974), pp. 3–34.

Hoffman, John C. *Ethical Confrontation in Counseling.* University of Chicago Press, 1979.

Lambert, Clinton E., Jr., and Lambert, Vickie A. "Divorce: A Psychodynamic Development Involving Grief." *Journal of Psychiatric Nursing,* Vol. 15, No. 1 (January 1977), pp. 37–42.

Lynch, James J. *The Broken Heart.* Basic Books, 1977.

McCormick, Richard A., S.J. "Divorce and Remarriage." *The Catholic Mind,* Vol. 73 (November 1975), pp. 42–57.

Peppler, Alice S. *Divorced and Christian.* Concordia Publishing House, 1974. Paperback.

Whelan, Charles M., S. J. "Divorced Catholics: A Proposal." *America,* Vol. 131 (December 7, 1974), pp. 363–365.

2. The Pastoral Care of Recovering Mental Patients

George Bennett has written a thorough guide for the family and the patient in his book entitled *When the Mental Patient Comes Home*. A thorough reading of his book by you and interested lay leaders will form a profound bond of understanding with the extended family in the care of convalescing mental patients. Bennett writes out of rich experience as a pastor, a mental-hospital chaplain, and a dean of students in a seminary. He has walked innumerable miles in the shoes of mental patients and their families. He wraps technical knowledge in the wisdom of clear and plain language. My purpose here is to provide technical data and suggestions for you as pastor.

The seriously disturbed mental patient, like the patient who has surgery, is spending less time in the hospital. Several reasons are behind this. The use of antipsychotic, antidepressant, and anxiety-relieving medications has reduced the need for acutely disturbed patients to stay under twenty-four-hour nursing care and custodial, closed-doors hospitalization. Furthermore, the legal basis on which anyone can be kept in the hospital involuntarily has been narrowed down to the hazards of suicide, homicide, or extreme psychotic behavior that threatens both the patient and the common good of the community.

In addition to these reasons, the federal government has set up comprehensive mental-health centers in cooperation with state governments all over the country. The patient is referred to these facilities, in which most of the ill are ambulatory outpatients.

Furthermore, the function of psychiatrists has shifted to a more biochemical management of patients. Psychotherapy is not the primary method of treatment; often the use of psychotropic medications is the only treatment. A considerable number of patients are cared for solely by general practitioners. Yet the more seriously disturbed psychotic and depressed patients still go to psychiatric hospitals in numbers large enough to be on waiting lists for beds. Eventually they are returned home to cope with life again and to get as much help as possible from their community. When this occurs, you, their pastor, and your congregation have the opportunity to provide kinds of care that will foresee and prevent a relapse during their convalescence.

THE CONVALESCENCE OF A MENTAL PATIENT: A LITTLE-USED RITUAL

The very idea of a mental patient needing a time of convalescence is rarely thought of. We say: "You are looking just great. You are your old self again. I guess you are eager to get back to work!" On the contrary, mental patients returning home have, like patients released after serious major surgery, a severely shaken self-confidence. They are still struggling to assimilate the events of their illness into a semblance of meaning and order. The trips back to the doctor for aftercare will be frequent enough to evoke wonder in them and a feeling of mystery. They may wonder if their employer will place them back on the job. The ever-present feeling of stigma is there. Consequently, there is need for a time of convalescence in which the patient's former routine is reestablished bit by bit. So it is better to say: "It is good to see you again. Take it easy and rebuild your program of work, worship, love, and play gradually. A step-by-step approach is best. I will be standing by and eager to talk with you as you gradually get back into action. If you get discouraged, remember that I am as near as your telephone."

The idea of convalescence also involves coaching the patient's family, who may not be aware of how long it takes to recuperate from the treatment and the side effects of such disorders as depression or schizophrenia. For example, specific medical advice is needed to determine when the patient should return to work. It is important to know whether the work involves operating machines, automobiles, or trucks, and whether the place of work is a happy one where the patient receives support and friendship from supervisors and fellow workers. Poignantly enough, the illness at its onset may have been related to the loss of a job. The church can work together quietly in seeing to it that a job is found. Schizophrenic patients too often drift from an adequate job to another of less value both in pay and satisfaction. Possibly the leadership of the church can quietly see to it that the patient has an opportunity to return to the same job or to find a job of equal pay and satisfaction.

Many patients from the four hospitals in which I serve simply have nowhere to go, no home to which to return. They may be completely alone in the world or have families who do not want them. Ideally, an inn or a halfway house or, as one in my city is called, The All-the-Way House, should be available to the people who have no other place to go. Sometimes our staff does not discharge a patient who is medically ready for discharge simply because there is no place for such a person to go. Churches can exercise major leadership by establishing, staffing, and maintaining residences where convalescing mental patients can have a home. Retired professional persons, high-school seniors, and college students could help maintain a program of natural friendships for these persons, who are shy, sad, withdrawn and sensitive, and are capable of friendship if it is extended to them and not quickly withdrawn. Churches often buy houses adjacent to their property in order to expand in new building programs. Could some of these houses be made into temporary quarters for discharged but homeless mental patients?

We could go one step farther. Increasingly younger persons are becoming psychiatric patients. They often come from homes where they are not wanted, and may actually have such hostile relationships with their biological families that a respite is strongly indicated. Such young persons really need a foster home for six months or a year. Could members of your church who are wisely motivated provide that home? If you have social workers in your congregation, they could supply technical assistance. In the case of students, if a school program needs attention, public school principals and teachers can give it.

This is a dream hard to realize. Think of it as your prayer, not only for the number of patients you have seen discharged but for the witness and work of the church you lead. If some young persons had the help of such a community before they fell ill, the illness itself would not be so severe and could often be handled by a physician without hospitalization.

The Importance of Psychiatric Medications

You will notice that convalescing mental patients are often on outpatient dosages of medications. When you see people who are seriously disturbed, ask what medicines they are taking. This includes prescription medications, over-the-counter "patent" medicines, and any illegal substances such as marijuana. Other chemical substances are important, too, such as alcohol, the caffeine in coffee and cola drinks, and the nicotine in cigars, pipe tobacco, and cigarettes. You may feel that to ask about these is to be "moralistic" and authoritarian. If you feel that way honestly, you would convey that impression. I do not feel that way, but rather put alcohol and tobacco along with all other harmful substances. I may even disclaim laying guilt upon patients by saying that my major concern is their health.

As for the medication for psychiatric illnesses, you may need a brief outline of their names and uses. They are classified into three groups: the antipsychotic or neuroleptic drugs, the antidepressant drugs, and the antianxiety drugs. Antipsychotic drugs are used primarily with patients who have presenting symptoms of hallucinations, delusions, and disorientation as to who they are, where they are, and what they are doing. These medications have a general classification name, phenothiazines. Some of their brand names are Thorazine, Stelazine, and Haldol. The antidepressants are not given one general classification with subtypes. Amitriptyline is one of the most commonly used antidepressants. It comes under such brand names as Elavil and Endep. Sometimes it is combined with anxiety-relieving drugs and has brand names such as Triavil or Limbitrol.

The anxiety-relieving agents are often variations of meprobamate, diazepam, etc. They come under brand names of Miltown, Valium, and Librium.

The outpatient on medications has several big problems:
1. The thought that it is a spiritual failure to have to take them.
2. The fear of neglecting or forgetting to take them.
3. The possibility of intentionally or unintentionally taking an overdose, and thus committing suicide.

4. The temptation to give or sell the medications to someone else.

Two long-acting medications have been developed, so that
a patient can take them by injection once every two or three
weeks. One, for persons diagnosed as schizophrenic, is Pro-
lixin; the other, for patients who are manic-depressive, is
lithium. Sometimes lithium is used with schizophrenic patients who also manifest considerable depression.

Your task as a pastor is to know these things about medications. A reading of Ross J. Baldessarini's *Chemotherapy in
Psychiatry* (Harvard University Press, 1977) gives detailed
information that you will find very useful. Furthermore, you
may know a few things about the medications, but since you
are not an authority, it is better to refer patients back to their
physicians, or even place the calls yourself. The best course
is to encourage the patient to follow the physician's orders.
Medications wisely used mean the employment of one part
of God's creation to put the imbalances in the patient's body
back into balance. If you detect misuse and abuse, or lack of
use, you can do a great service to the patient to ask for the
privilege of speaking to the physician in charge of the case.

ELECTRIC CONVULSIVE THERAPY

Electric convulsive therapy, commonly called shock therapy, is still widely used, especially in treating depression in
middle-aged men and women. I am told that it is most often
indicated for depressed persons aged about forty-five to fifty-
five who have not previously suffered from depression. In one
of the hospitals where I work regularly, only an occasional
patient receives this kind of treatment. In another of my
hospitals, it is never used at all. When it is used, I have
noticed that the patient sleeps deeply. Sleep is greatly needed.
Also, I have noted a temporary but extensive loss of memory.

Some studies indicate that minimal memory loss persists. My own pastoral observations dwell on the terror patients feel for this treatment, the way they tend to look upon it as punishment or even electrocution. Highly educated persons who depend heavily on their memories know that the treatment does impair memory. Thus they resist it.

Yet one of the crippling aspects of depression is the way the patient ruminates over past events. Some forgetting is an outright necessity. Hence shock therapy, used with a highly selected number of patients, is efficacious. However, it should not be used in desperation when nothing else does any good. Nor should it be used as an expression of the physician's impatience with a difficult case.

Your Relationship to the Physicians

If I were with you in a pastors' workshop, you might readily say: "You may be able to do all these things where you are, but the physicians in my territory won't talk with me about anything. They are just not cooperative." I can say: "You are right, but something can be done about that in a personal way. Examine your own relationship to those physicians. Are you defensive with them? If so, they will be defensive in return. Introduce yourself personally to them when you are in the hospital area, or when you see them in other settings. Send patients to them with a letter of referral. Invite them to speak before church and community groups you are sponsoring. Acts of friendship beget acts of friendship."

As a group, you and the other ministers in your area can collaborate with the local medical society in religion and health workshops. Physicians like to work in these if they have a part in developing and planning the programs. In fact, I have participated in such programs initiated by physicians themselves. But such understanding does not just happen; it requires disciplined work over a period of years by more than one minister.

SOME GUIDELINES FOR COUNSELING WITH RECOVERING MENTAL PATIENTS

Here are specific suggestions on how to counsel with recovering mental patients:

1. On the first interview, encourage them to tell you what they think you need to know about their experience in the hospital. Then declare that you consider all this to be in the past and want them to talk about it whenever they need to, but always in the past tense. Don't permit interminable rehashing of any one subject or occurrence. Simply say that you listened closely to what they said about that and remember it well. Rehashing may do no harm but it does not advance them toward here-and-now living.

2. Encourage them to ventilate the uneasiness they feel toward family, friends, the church and you. Be careful not to overreassure or overpromise. Promise little; do much.

3. Let them feel free to set their own pace in getting back into the activities of the church, but insist that they set a time, however tentative, for doing so. Large crowds may make them feel conspicuous, but a very large crowd may provide them enough privacy to feel at ease. The socializing before and after services of worship makes many persons nervous, and mental patients are no exception. If you seat them in a spot where they could leave whenever they choose, they know that you do not intend to trap them. It may well be that joining a small group, such as a weekday evening Bible-study group or a Sunday school class, is the best course for a while.

4. Do what you can to prevent their family and friends from harping on the illness. They do not understand their

own need to keep the patient helpless. For example, one family, husband and adult sons and daughters, made a habit of waiting on the ailing mother hand and foot. She was quite able to care for herself and did so when a clear understanding was developed in the family. It seems that the husband had more or less enjoyed the sympathy he got from the larger community because his wife was an "invalid" mental patient. A play on the word "invalid" shifted their thinking to assuming that she was *valid,* not *in* valid. She responded and ceased to live a helpless life. She became the fully functioning adult that she really is.

5. Do not wait for a crisis to visit the patient and the family. Plan to see them once a week for the first month if they agree; then see them once a month. We know that schizophrenic patients tend to become depressed after returning home. So common is this that some physicians call it the PPD—the postpsychotic depression. Rough estimates suggest that this occurs in 25 percent of the cases. (McGlashan and Carpenter, "Post Psychotic Depression in Schizophrenia," *Archives of General Psychiatry,* Vol. 33, February 1976, pp. 231–39). Spending a half hour once a week for four or five weeks with such patients puts you in position to detect the onset of sadness and encourage them to convey this to their doctor. You might help by asking permission to call the doctor yourself. One great drawback during an attack of depression is the loss of initiative.

These are some working guidelines for you as a pastor. You will find that George Bennett's book, *When the Mental Patient Comes Home,* constitutes a useful guide for either the family or the patient. On your next contact with them, you can deal with any questions they raise about the book's suggestions. Bennett's book also gives wholesome advice for dealing with all people.

The Use of Groups

Two nationwide organizations devote themselves to enabling people to get back into action after a mental disorder. Recovery, Inc. is a long-standing group, with national offices at 116 South Michigan Avenue, Chicago, Illinois 60003. The branch in my city can be addressed at P. O. Box 5645, and its office is at 2022 Bonnycastle Avenue, Louisville, Kentucky 40205. If there is a branch in your area, look it up in your telephone directory. Emotions Anonymous is a newer and less well known group, and it works on some of the same principles as Alcoholics Anonymous. Of course, many mental disorders are directly related to the sustained abuse of alcohol. Toxic conditions such as Korsakoff's syndrome and Wernicke's syndrome are specific alcohol-related problems. Such sufferers can be aided greatly by Alcoholics Anonymous, Al-Anon, or Alateen.

However, you may want to organize a group of your own church members who need the support of others in their lives. A group of eight or ten can be most helpful. One way of leading such a group would be to use George Bennett's book as a guide for study. Furthermore, growth groups such as Howard J. Clinebell suggests in *The People Dynamic* (Harper & Row, 1972) would go far toward preventing mental disorders or reducing their severity. If someone must be hospitalized, then the group will be on hand to provide assistance when the patient is discharged.

The Prevention of Mental Disorders

You and I as Christians must not be too global in our claims that a healthy faith in God will prevent all mental disorders. Our task as teachers of personal moral and spiritual values can do much to prevent or ease some mental disorders. Despite our best efforts, however, some persons will suffer psychotic breakdowns. We can be a part of anticipating the breaks with reality and seeing to it that the attendant stigma, shame, and isolation are removed or reduced. Furthermore, you are in a pastoral position to observe and listen to the stresses that go with the common crises of life—birth, puberty, turning the eighteenth birthday, the death of a spouse, the loss of a job, retirement, and so on.

One of the best ways to prevent mental illness is by helping people to establish clear-cut goals for living. Having a definite mission with a commonsense faith in God helps people in the face of stress. The development of skills that make young persons self-supporting in work that they enjoy helps to ward off the malaise that overtakes purposeless people. Challenging the temptations to idolatry in those who are broken-hearted as a result of death, divorce, or the defection of a loved one helps them to get on with life. Even so, some people languish in grief, guilt, and hopelessness because they think their lives are over when they lose someone, or when the child-rearing period comes to an end.

The Christian gospel lays great value upon the family. At the same time it subordinates the family to a larger loyalty to the Kingdom of Heaven. The Christian community is called to communicate a new life and purpose for living in Jesus Christ. At its best, the Christian community reaches out to the desolate—to widows, fatherless persons, and others like Nicodemus and the Gadarene demoniac. Jesus sent the demoniac back to his home city to witness to the people. I hope that when he got there he found a pastor like you, who is concerned about enabling the former mental patient to become active again in his own community.

Suggestions for Further Reading

Caplan, Gerald. *Principles of Preventive Psychiatry.* Basic Books, 1964.

Erickson, Gerald D., and Hogan, Terrence P. *Family Therapy: An Introduction to Theory and Technique.* Jason Aronson, 1976.

Oates, Wayne E. *The Religious Care of the Psychiatric Patient.* Westminster Press, 1978.

Pincus, J. H., and Tucker, G. J. *Behavioral Neurology.* Oxford University Press, 1978.

Schuyler, Dean. *The Depressive Spectrum.* Jason Aronson, 1974.

Usdin, Gene. *Schizophrenia: Biological and Psychological Perspectives.* Brunner-Mazel, 1975.

3. The Pastoral Care of Those in Perpetual Sorrow

Jan Cox-Gedmark, chaplain at the Institute of Physical Medicine and Rehabilitation, Louisville, Kentucky, has written *Coping with Physical Disability,* the Westminster Christian Care Book addressed to those who are in continual or perpetual grief because of severe handicaps of body or mind. They and their family members may be expected to live a normal life-span; they cannot anticipate an early end to the life of the afflicted. However, for such persons to live, their families must give them huge parts of their own lives. The handicap may be mental retardation, blindness or deafness (or both), paralysis—partial or complete—due to trauma from industrial, automobile, or sports accidents or cardiovascular strokes, massive war wounds, or such causes of grief as knowing that a relative is missing in action. Long-term illnesses such as multiple sclerosis, diabetes, hemophilia, hemochromatosis, and others also plunge individuals and families into chronic sorrowing.

THE CONCEPT OF PERPETUAL OR "NO END" GRIEF

One of the lessons learned from combat studies of stress is that it can be borne more easily, and more of it can be borne

56

with greater equanimity, if the person being stressed knows when it will be over (Peter G. Bourne, *Men, Stress, and Vietnam*, pp. 63–81; Little, Brown & Co., 1970). With "no end in sight," the grief becomes a perpetual or chronic sorrow. Simon Olshansky relates this concept to the feelings of parents who have a mentally defective child. He says that this kind of sorrow has not always been recognized by professionals. This "blind spot" causes the professional to make serious mistakes in the caring process. These mistakes can be enumerated:

1. Professionals tend to belabor "the tendency of the parent to deny the reality of the child's mental deficiency."

2. Professionals tend to view chronic sorrow as a neurotic manifestation rather than a natural and understandable response to a tragic fact.

3. Professionals impatiently push parents for greater and greater acceptance of the tragedy in spite of the periodic exhaustion of their emotional reserves. "Some parents may require months, or even years, of counseling before they can muster and maintain the strength and stamina needed to live with the tragedy of having a mentally defective child." (Simon Olshansky, "Chronic Sorrow: A Response to Having a Mentally Defective Child," *Social Casework*, Vol. 43, 1962, pp. 190–193.)

Another observer of "no end" grief, John G. Bruhn, Ph.D., considers the effects of one member's chronic illness on the rest of the family. Doctor Bruhn says that the usual ways in which family members interact with each other are disrupted and the equilibrium of the family is disturbed by the unchanging fact of the illness or handicap of one member. Caretaking duties are shifted from one who experiences the illness as a loss to another who considers it a burden. Old symptoms in other members of the family are renewed and new symptoms appear. In this interaction "a sick member may become sicker" and "well members may become sick to call attention to themselves or the need to reallocate tasks, especially if they feel themselves overshadowed or overburdened by the ill family member."

Bruhn further cites evidence from larger population studies to the effect that with severe chronic diseases such as diabetes mellitus, hemophilia, and epilepsy "the rate of family breakdown is high." If the demands for change created by the illness cannot be met, the family disintegrates in divorce or abandonment. "The chronically ill child," says Bruhn, "may be the 'lightning rod' for marital and family problems, so his and his family's adjustment to the illness is further complicated."

The routines, the family rituals, and the times of celebration in a family with a chronically handicapped member all tend to evoke either heroic efforts at renewal of morale or increased emotional lability, depression, and irritability. Even caring for the patient can become a tug of war as to which relative calls the most, who has the most intimate access to the patient's confidence, or who is most neglectful. You as a pastor may be caught in the strain of these emotional crosscurrents. (John G. Bruhn, "Effects of Chronic Illness on the Family," *The Journal of Family Practice*, Vol. 4, No. 6, June 1977, pp. 1057–1060.)

You as a pastor are also concerned with descriptive diagnoses such as Olshansky and Bruhn provide. They help you understand what is going on within a family in chronic grief over the chronic illness or handicap of one of its members. Yet this serves only as helpful background for you. Your principal concern is the vertical relationship of all the members of this family to God and their interspersing relationship to the extended family of the church.

THE FAMILY'S RELATIONSHIP TO GOD

The chronically sorrowing family may reflect any one or more of a spectrum of feelings and attitudes toward God. Let me discuss a few that I have observed clinically.

First, the family may feel that if God chooses, God will perform a miracle and bring this sorrow to an end by curing, healing, or bestowing special overcoming strength to their stricken loved one. I have always felt that this kind of hope is to expect magic of God and to manipulate him—literally, to put God to the test. In Luke 4:9–12, Jesus was tempted by the devil to put God to the test by casting himself down from the pinnacle of the Temple, to prove that he would not be hurt. Jesus refused to yield to the desire to be an exception to the laws of gravity and human limitations. I must continue, therefore, to rule out the magical wish to evade the laws of nature.

However, once I have explained this interpretation, I must add that I think that persons who are in chronic sorrow are often asking the question of God asked by the psalmists and the prophets again and again: "How long, O Lord, how long?" They are praying for relief—"Come *quickly*, Lord, I've stood all I can take!" The prayer, furthermore, is at heart a confession of helplessness: "I've done all I can, Lord. I am exhausted. Please perform a miracle."

The prayer for a miracle is the cry of the desperate. We have a right before God to ask for a miracle, but to dictate the terms of God's miracle is to miss the opportunity of seeing the miracle that God in his infinite wisdom may be about to perform. The miracle may be the healing of the chronically ill one. It may be the revelation and discovery of new ways of treating the illness. In this way, not just this person but hundreds and thousands of others later will be healed. The miracle may be an increase of patience, courage, and renewal in the one who prays. Whatever the miracle is, I make bold to believe that everyone has the right and should be encouraged to ask for one—but without putting conditions upon God, who is unconditional Love.

Second, the perpetually sorrowing family may be "perplexed before God." The state of mind is not one of depression. The apostle Paul said, "We are . . . perplexed, yet not driven to despair" (II Cor. 4:8). The father of a severely retarded daughter is a faithful Catholic, one who perceives the daughter as a gift from God. He sees himself and her mother as being "specially called" to care for this gift. Yet he and the mother are financially drained by the cost of special education for the child. They are heavily in debt. He says: "I know that God gave us this child, but I can't understand why he does not open ways for us to pay all these bills." When one "can't understand," one is perplexed. You and I as pastors get quickly to the heart of a family's suffering when we ask someone like this man what he feels about God. We can take part in mobilizing the resources of the church and the larger community to redistribute both the personal and the financial demand on this couple. And we need not let our left hand know what our right hand is doing. We are perplexed, too. We can pray in secret for an "opening," an imaginative plan, a practical solution to the perplexing question this man raises. We can admit our own perplexity to the person. We can commit ourselves to composing a *Guide for the Perplexed*, as Moses Maimonides called his great philosophical work. But this man does not need an exposition of the "goodness and severity of God," although that is about what he is experiencing as he frames his perplexity into words. What he needs is fellowship in his perplexity, and you can supply that. What he needs is company in his courageous search for ways of caring for his daughter. You can be that company. The church, the body of Christ, can provide much more company than you alone can if they are adequately sensitized to the need. In community agencies there are many more people who can speak and do things that enable this man and woman to do what they feel "specially called" to do.

A third problem the family that chronically sorrows addresses to God in your presence is the question: "What have I done that this should befall my son (my daughter, my husband, my wife, as the case may be)?" A policeman is injured in an automobile accident while pursuing bank thieves. He is permanently paralyzed from his waist down, confined to a wheelchair. His wife—against all efforts to relieve her—stands watch at the hospital day after day, week after week. She does not sleep much except for naps in a chair. She eats very little. She hovers over her husband. She anxiously awaits each new medical report on the extent of damage to his body, watches measures prescribed to increase the use of his body, and hears estimates of his chances for recovery. She berates herself for her own part in causing his handicap. She asks her pastor: "Why is God punishing us like this?"

You as a pastor can be too reassuring at this point. Once I asked a man with tuberculosis, who told me his sin had caused his illness: "Do you have any idea of what you might have done?" He did. He said that he had been greedy at work. He had snatched at every chance for overtime and had worked day and night, seven days a week for years. Now it was finally catching up with him. He even said: "The Lord has made me lie down, as it says in the Twenty-third psalm." This man taught me much. The pastoral principle I learned was to take everyone seriously in reality; they may have something specific to tell, to "disburden" as Max Thurian calls it in his book, *Confession* (SCM Press, 1958). Such a question may be the opening sentence of a private confessional. Too hasty reassurance snuffs out this light. Your response may veer the conversation into abstractions, classroom theodicies, and frustrated communication for both of you.

Yet let us assume that as a pastor you have listened carefully to the words of what people say they may have done to cause God to do this to them. You will do well to explore also their relationship to others. For example, you may ask: "Has anyone you know accused you of having done something to earn the disfavor of God?" I have asked this question and the answer revealed that a parent, a brother or sister, or a parent-in-law had said such things as this: "Well, I told you when you two were living together before you were married that God would punish you. This is it." Or, "I told you that you were marrying into a bad line of people and that it would show up in your children." Or, "After all the trouble you've given me, now you are getting your share."

These are curses that people half believe and also impute to God. You as a pastor have the task of separating the harsh judgments of human beings from the wisdom and mercy of God. In a sense, their perception of God has been distorted and obscured by the harsh authority of parents and other family members. A frank statement such as this is not out of place: "Your parent may feel just this way. However, that person is not God. You need to consult God for your own self in your prayers and in the study of the Scriptures. May I be your guide in that? You have a right to your own relationship to God. I promise you I will not be unfaithful to God or to you." You remember that these people need the relatives they quote and that you must not further alienate them. You can be an effective pastor to them, but you cannot take the place of their family members.

Maybe you will have an opportunity to be a minister of reconciliation if you have access to the anguished relative who *allegedly* said such things. Yet you have already undertaken to disentangle the complainer's sense of rejection by God and to focus it on a rejection, real or imagined, by the complainer's family. With an adequate pastoral blessing, you remove the alienation and "curse" imputed to God and communicate the affection, acceptance, and love of God.

However, your complainers may not have anything so specific in mind as a rejection by parents and other family members. To the contrary, when you explore their religious history you may find a remarkable sense of deprivation that dates back to their earliest days. They believe that they have been repeatedly abandoned. They have not had the nurturing fellowship of a caring church. They have known discouragement after discouragement, failure after failure. This is the most recent one—having a handicapped child, or a family member permanently disabled by an industrial accident. Their question: "What have I done to deserve *this?*" simply climaxes a long train of events that have beset them. They seem to be saying, not that they have done something displeasing to God but that they evidently merit no favor in the eyes of God or other people. Here you as a pastor are meeting their sense of personal worthlessness, of being of no value. Through taking their feelings about God seriously, you have come upon their desolation—their feeling of being "orphaned"—and their poverty-stricken self-image. You can involve them in a nurturing growth group. You can introduce them to a fellowship group that has similar problems but more family support. You can introduce them to an older couple, perhaps grandparents whose sons and daughters have married and left home. All these can mutually encourage and believe in each other. You yourself can see the wavering ones periodically, because just doing so assures them they are worthy of your interest. They have trouble believing this, but the fact is there. You can value them. You can "show *and* tell" them that God values them. Emotionally deprived persons need regular spiritual restoration of repeatedly withdrawn personal valuation normally given and always expected and hoped for by all of us.

PERSISTENT TEMPTATIONS OF THE CHRONIC SORROWER

As Jan Cox-Gedmark has said in her book, there is "no end" to the sorrow that persons such as we are discussing here experience. Life is lived in a sense of hope when circumstances change, when the sufferer can measure progress by specific improvements. When there is no change, one must bide one's time until the end of one's suffering is fulfilled. That "end" is death. Little wonder is it that persons with a permanent illness or injury will ask: "Why can't I die?" and that those who have primary responsibility as family members will ask the same questions about their charges. The very thought of such words is so terrifying that one stifles them back from consciousness. For to admit them into one's mind is to be faced with three temptations at least.

First is the temptation to give up and contemplate suicide: "I'd be better off dead." The shock of such a thought is horrifying and held to one's inner counsels as incommunicable to others. If you as a pastor are aware of this as a temptation, then people may confide in you as a confessor that this thought bothers them. The very act of sharing it with you reduces the possibility that it will happen. Furthermore, you will recognize this as a symptom of depression and encourage your counselees to confide also in their physician. This further insulates them from acting on impulse and puts the despair of life into a nonjudgmental frame. That despair is the last bastion of defense against accepting the harsh reality of the handicap or illness. This dark time comes just before the dawning of an acceptance that spurs afflicted persons on to look for ways of gathering their remaining strengths so as to make the most of the rest of life. Furthermore, the appearance of this temptation is a signal for you to increase the frequency of your visits and telephone calls to these persons, and thereby giving them something specific toward which to look forward.

A second temptation is to abandon the loved one who is chronically ill or handicapped. Public-hospital staffs are well acquainted with the phenomenon of finding such persons in the waiting rooms or parking lots, left there by relatives. Often the successful placing of patients in a hospital becomes a time for their relatives to abandon them.

A third temptation is that of either passively neglecting persons who are ill or handicapped until they die, or actively doing something that will end their lives.

The pain of such thoughts is something you may wisely choose not to bring up in conversation. Yet knowing that these thoughts lurk in the hinterlands of consciousness, or crowd the forehead of awareness in the persons with whom you work, keeps you alertly on the watch for the temptations to emerge in the confessions you hear. To hear them as temptations, not sins, is important. Theologically, we do not allow much room in our confessional ministry for a marked difference between sin and temptation. You can thank God with those making confession that they have had the confidence in you and the courage before God to acknowledge the temptations in their hearts. We have a high priest in Jesus Christ who joins us as we boldly approach the throne of grace to find help in time of need.

The Family's Relationship to the Community of Faith

You rightly feel drained from dealing with families who are chronically sorrowing. What you feel is exactly what the perpetually grieving family members feel, but with greater intensity. Yet you cannot bear all these people's burdens alone. Your sense of solitariness bespeaks the very need of the transformation of the church of which you are pastor into a fellowship of concern and outreach to persons in all stations of life. Especially needy are these chronically sorrowing families in which a member lives with irreversible handicaps from birth or accident or crippling disorders.

Support Groups

Periodically I have had the privilege of visiting churches that have organized groups of persons whose sons or daughters are mentally retarded. These parents provide each other with emotional support, a steady exchange of helpful information, and the encouragement to keep working creatively to make their concerns develop human character rather than to destroy it. They serve as a social-change group that educates other families who do not have retarded children. They ask for special programs for their children in the church and community. They bear their witness to the power of the Lord Jesus Christ to make difficulties like this serve the larger interests of the Kingdom of Heaven. Governmental services for these families can be increased and improved by the lobbying efforts of such a group. Thus the grief the families feel can be mobilized into action that slackens the power of the grief to dominate the families' whole life. Isolation is done away with by such groups.

Groups, however, do not have to be made up exclusively of handicapped persons and their families. It is also possible to merge their group participation into the mainstream of church life. This is done by sensitizing and informing the already existing natural groups of the church to the special needs of the chronically ill, the perpetually sorrowing, and the permanently handicapped. A Sunday school class, a youth group, or a choir, for example, will make a special effort to include them, or to reach out to them if they cannot attend and participate. Different groups may take responsibility for making cassette tapes to take to the home of the afflicted, while others can arrange a schedule of volunteers for sit-in duty, thus relieving the family members for a while, to shop, to attend church, or to catch up on duties put off.

Both the specialized groups and the mainstreaming arrangements are needed. They need not be exclusive of each other, since each will meet some persons' needs better.

Some Tangible Things Can Be Done

Families with handicapped members often feel neglected by "the passing show" of people who have not been affected as they have. They feel that their daily routine and their preoccupations with neverending responsibilities place them in another world. A few very tangible things can be done to let them know that they live in the same world with you as their pastor and the church as their church.

1. *Parking places near the entrances,* displaying the wheelchair symbol of the handicapped, can be reserved for them. This makes the distance they have to travel from a car much shorter.

2. *Ramps at curbs and at steps* can be constructed inexpensively in existing structures. When new buildings are planned, ramps should be included. Thus persons in wheelchairs can be more independent and less conspicuous in a gathering crowd. And anyone who has difficulty walking can manage better on a ramp than on steps.

3. *Elevators* provide a special blessing for handicapped persons and their families. They eliminate some of the need for ramps.

These are tangible, nonverbal ways of conveying the good news: "We have been waiting for you and expecting you. We have made special arrangements for you. You are especially welcome here!" When these quiet communicators of care are lacking, negative or bad news is communicated.

THE ORDINANCES OR SACRAMENTS

Let me suggest that handicapped persons and their families be provided Communion at home. To do this, gather a company of persons of the church who know a family and its handicapped person fairly well, and meet at their home to "observe the Lord's Supper" or "administer Holy Communion," as you would describe it in keeping with your faith and tradition. The mystical depths of the nonverbal community thus created give an eternal "now" moment in this family's life. Thus God refreshes his people "on their toilsome way." The toilsomeness of perpetual sorrow places the tribulations of time in the context of a larger suffering of the death, burial, and resurrection of our Lord Jesus Christ.

We often overlook the power of music to give fresh strength to the "weary and heavy laden." A youth group can join you as you go to the home of one of their fellow high school or college mates who, let us say, has been paralyzed from the waist down in a football accident. They can sing, play their guitars, and bring new hope for the living of these days to both the injured-for-life young man and his grieving family.

CAN THESE SOURCES OF SORROW BE PREVENTED?

Prophet witness is stirred when you see a young person with permanent brain damage resulting from a motorcycle accident. Holy horror at unsafe automobiles and careless or reckless driving wells up in you when you see someone doomed to suffer permanently from extensive burns, yet amazingly spared to live a reasonably long life. Industrial accidents and diseases prompt a fresh qualm of conscience about safety measures in industries within your parish. Also, when you see a Down's syndrome, or Mongoloid, child you ask: "Can these things be prevented?" A great many of them could be prevented. That is the answer, and it poses a new challenge to you as a preacher, an agent of social change, and an organizer.

As a preacher, the basic perennial task of educating people in handling automobiles is an ethical responsibility. Nearly 50,000 persons a year die in automobile accidents, but 7,000,000 are injured, many of them permanently. You can raise the consciousness of your people by insisting that a part of your church teaching program be focused on the ethical challenges implicit in owning and driving automobiles. At the periodic crises over the availability of gasoline, the attention of people is on their cars. At the sixteenth birthdays, families hover anxiously around the new driver who is getting access to car keys. One pastor formulated a "Litany of the Keys" as a medium of instruction about the use of cars.

Furthermore, in sermons, you as a pastor can periodically build a conscience about television viewing. Many of the police stories on the screen are filled with violent uses of automobiles. Screeching tires, burning cars, impossible traffic behavior, crashing of cars into each other are steady eye and ear diet. Is this what your congregation and you want to see? If not, say so! Write letters to the producers, the networks, and—most especially—the companies whose advertisements support these shows.

A good antidote is to provide at the same time a preview guide for the best TV viewing scheduled. Many highly creative and rightly motivated programs can be recommended. A panel from your congregation can be enlisted to make this selection each week, or several panels can take turns at it. A set of criteria for selection can be developed and tested by succeeding panels. It is not good enough just to cry "awful" about bad TV. We need to find and encourage what is praiseworthy in a medium that is here to stay.

Many genetically determined handicaps can be predicted on the basis of chromosome studies. You can refer the expectant mother who has had a retarded child to a diagnostic and evaluation center in a university medical school. My colleague, Bernard Weisskopf, M.D., advises that the test known as amniocentesis is a procedure in which fluid is drawn from the amniotic sac of an expectant mother. Extensive laboratory study of this fluid provides an analysis of the chromosomes. Defects can be identified within the time of pregnancy, which can then be interrupted if the prospective infant will be abnormal. Professor Weisskopf suggests the following criteria for the use of the amniocentesis procedure:

1. Maternal age over thirty-five. (At age thirty-five the incidence of Down's syndrome is about 1 percent. After thirty-five the incidence increases dramatically.)
2. A parent with known chromosomal aberrations.
3. A previous child with chromosomal abnormalities.
4. A family history of metabolic disorder.

(Nature, through spontaneous abortion or miscarriage, prevents half of these potential births.)

However, you as a pastor have a responsibility to assess the ethical convictions of the couple involved. If they have profound convictions opposing abortion, then they simply are going through a great deal of stress to find out something they cannot in conscience do anything about. This ethical dilemma can be foiled ahead of time. The information I have given here is in the public mind through television and the news media. If you are asked about amniocentesis by a couple, I would suggest close collaboration with the physicians of the mother-to-be. However, the background knowledge presented here is important to keep in mind.

THE PROPHETIC ISSUES IN INDUSTRIAL HEALTH AND SAFETY

The critical challenge posed by violations of industrial health and safety rules calls for pastoral wisdom applied in careful observation, case follow-ups, and much discipline of one's sense of indignation. Mining accidents, black lung from coal mines, pneumoconiosis from working with cement, and brown lung from working in cotton mills are examples of widespread health hazards that cripple and maim workers in such occupations.

Your situation is ambiguous in that owners and managers of mines, plants, and mills may well be members of your congregation, and being an advocate for the employees puts you in the position of a petitioner. You walk a narrow ridge of prophetic necessity to appeal to these executives on behalf of the workers. However, you are in communication with both the handicapped employers and the need for compassion and willingness to curb profits for the sake of health and safety in their industries.

The whole situation may be such as to make you feel that you are attacking an elephant with a penknife. Yet one profound conversation with one decision maker, in which you appeal to him in the name and Spirit of the Lord Jesus Christ, may result in preventing thousands of crippling accidents and cases of disease. One carefully prayed through and disciplined utterance in a sermon may well bring the whole issue to a level of consciousness that will prompt community comradeship in changing a whole industry. Patient participation on a committee for health and safety may be less dramatic, but in the long pull do as much good. Pastoral care and social action blend in purpose and method here. The case method of pastoral care is the microlaboratory for identifying precisely the nature of the macroscopic social injustices. Such microscopic study makes your prophetic witness precise and rhetoric free, a double gift of the grace of God.

Suggestions for Further Reading

Bruhn, John G. "Effects of Chronic Illness on the Family." *The Journal of Family Practice*, Vol. 4, No. 6 (June 1977), pp. 1057–1060.

Martin, Maurice J. "Introduction: Psychiatric Aspects of Chronic Illness," and Krupp, Neal E., "Symposium: Adaptation to Chronic Illness." *Postgraduate Medicine*, Vol. 60, No. 5 (November 1976), pp. 121–125.

Olshansky, Simon. "Chronic Sorrow: A Response to Having a Mentally Defective Child." *Social Casework*, Vol. 43 (1962), pp. 190–193.

Pfefferbaum, Betty, and Pasnau, Robert O. "Post-Amputation Grief." *Nursing Clinics of North America*, Vol. 2, No. 4 (December 1976), pp. 687–690.

Schoenberg, Bernard; Gerber, Irwin; Wiener, Alfred; Kutscher, Austin H.; Peretz, David; and Carr, Arthur C., editors. *Bereavement: Its Psychosocial Aspects.* Columbia University Press, 1975.

Tenbrinck, Margaret S., and Brewer, Paul W. "The Stages of Grief Experienced by Parents of Handicapped Children." *Arizona Medicine*, Vol. 33, No. 9 (September 1976), pp. 712–714.

4. The Pastoral Care of Families in the Aftermath of Suicide

You as a pastor, along with members of your congregation, become an "aftermath team" who cares for a family when one of its members has committed suicide. John Hewett has written the book *After Suicide.* You will find that this book is one of the very few if not the only book written on this difficult subject to be handed to family members who have lost someone by suicide.

You may rightly ask: "Is suicide becoming more prevalent?" Therefore, let us look at some of the statistics on this subject.

THE INCIDENCE AND PREVALENCE OF SUICIDE

In the United States in 1975, the rate of suicide per 100,000 population was 12.7. In 1960 the rate was 10.6 per 100,000. The sex and age ratios of suicides in 1975 appear in the following groupings:

MALES

Ages 15–24—18.9 per 100,000
25–44—24.0 per 100,000
45–64—28.9 per 100,000
65 & above—36.8 per 100,000

FEMALES

Ages   15–24—4.8 per 100,000
25–44—9.9 per 100,000
45–64—11.9 per 100,000
65 & above—8.0 per 100,000

The shifts in rates of suicide from age group to age group are dramatic. Our culture's emphasis on youth as a prime value appears in the high incidence of suicide among men past the age of sixty-five and in the increase of suicides by women between the ages of forty-five and sixty-four. The rates of suicide among children and adolescents are comparatively low; but suicide and accidents, especially automobile accidents, are top causes of death among children and youth.

Your programs of prevention could be aimed at three groups of persons who tend to give up attending church: late adolescents, parents whose children are grown and have left home, and people above the age of sixty-five. The importance of these ages for a search for new meaning and identity in people's lives makes them an unusually needy group. They need your encouragement and mine to renew their lives in Jesus Christ's promise that in him we may have life and have life more abundantly. The struggle is a matter of life and death for those who can find no other solution of life's dilemmas, and their feeling of personal worthlessness, except suicide. Suicidal persons perceive themselves to be trapped in a "no exit" situation. Suicide is their exit, always available.

You can reach out and establish good communication with those who actually signal that they are in trouble by abandoning a moderately or exceptionally active church life for no visible cause. As Helmut Thielicke says, "There are many suicides—not because people have too little money or suffer disappointments in love—but because they lost the meaning of life and see themselves confronted by a black wall " (*The Faith Letters*, p. 7; Word Books, 1978).

THE FIRST PASTORAL VISIT

If you and your congregation are even remotely related to a family in which one of its members has just committed suicide, you are likely to be among the first they call. You go immediately, as you would in response to any other death call. Upon arrival at the scene, you are likely to find that the police are there or are on their way. A violent death has occurred and the legal establishment of the cause of death is imperative. A coroner's inquest is usual, and the body is removed only after the police have gathered and made a record of the evidence: suicide notes, empty drug containers, the gun if one was used, and so on.

These data are of great importance because the family will have a hard enough time believing that suicide was the cause of death, even when the evidence is unmistakable. For example, a twenty-five-year-old single woman left home after a quarrel with her parents. She was not heard of again for seven or eight months. Then the police notified her parents that they had found her body, badly decomposed, in a remote wooded area. Whether she was killed by someone else, died of natural causes, or committed suicide with an overdose of drugs is still a mystery. Legally, she is listed as a suicide. Her parents have no clear way of knowing. For them, grieving itself is complicated and hindered in its progress toward recovery.

Recovering the body of the deceased—as in cases of suicide by drowning—may be one of the most traumatic aspects of a death by suicide. Another traumatic feature is the sometimes grisly, horrid appearance of the body upon its discovery by the family. A ten-year-old girl comes home from school and finds her father dead in the bathroom, stained with blood. A couple returns from vacation to find their son's body partly decomposed in a car in the garage; he had used carbon-monoxide fumes to kill himself.

If you as a pastor are called in on such a situation, you may expect to help clean up these gruesome conditions even as you try to stabilize the panic and hysteria of the deceased's family, who will suffer for some time afterward whenever the first sight of the body flashes back into their consciousness.

One very important reason for a definite legal determination of the cause of death is that many insurance companies will pay to the beneficiary only the actual amount paid in by the deceased, not the face amount of the policy, if the death was a suicide. This fact is another jarring reality for the family to absorb.

The initial reactions of the family are highly unpredictable. Some typical responses are: "Why did you have to do such a thing to me and the children?" "The poor man, he just worked until he couldn't stand any more." "She didn't mean to do this. It was an accident." "It was not suicide. Someone broke into the house, shot him, and made it look like a suicide." "He came by the house. He showed me a gun. I hadn't the slightest idea this would happen." "What did I do wrong?" Injustice. Frustration. Hurt. Guilt. Anger. These are emotions that tumble pell-mell over each other in unrehearsed, unguarded first responses.

My policy is to encourage the flow of these emotions while the hurt is fresh. I like each individual to have as much privacy of expression as possible. Social conventions of meeting many people soon close over the wound. Rationalizations —some of which are absurd—take over quickly. You are likely to get a candid-camera view of the inner life of the surviving relatives in these first reactions. If good diagnosis is a part of all good therapy, and I think it is, you receive important clues to the relatives' deepest needs in the process of being a faithful and steadfast pastor to them as they "pour out their complaint before the Lord" in your hearing.

QUESTIONS YOU MAY BE ASKED

Certain questions are often asked about the death of one's family member by suicide. A review of some of these will enable you to be forearmed:

"Was sickness the cause?" This is asked in many ways, but basically they mean the same. The grief-stricken will ask: "Was it mental illness?" "Was it insanity?" "Was it the cancer, heart disease, medical disability that brought on a feeling that life was over?" At base is the effort to make the act of suicide make sense. Furthermore, a deeper concern is to absolve the suicide of responsibility. You as a person of God are in a sense being asked to bestow a by-proxy absolution.

We do know clinically that a clinical or vegetatively based depression, if untreated, can very often result in suicide. We also know that about one out of four schizophrenic patients, on recovery from a psychotic state, tends to become depressed and suicidal. Therefore, you may ask such questions as these to assess the presence or absence of depression before the suicide:

1. Had the person been hospitalized for terminal cancer, severe emphysema, a schizophrenic psychotic attack, a depression?
2. Did the person have severe trouble sleeping, especially awakening for no external cause very early in the morning and being unable to go back to sleep?
3. Had the person withdrawn from accustomed social, civic, work-related, or church-related activities? In other words, was the initiative impaired?

4. Did the person have persistent and uncontrollable crying spells?
5. Was there a loss of interest and ability in sexual relations with the spouse?
6. Did the person express self-derogatory comments such as "being tired of living," "being in the way of others," "not knowing how much longer it will be possible to stand the way things are"; or say, "I feel that I have sinned away the days of grace," "I have committed the unpardonable sin," or "The Spirit of God has left me"?
7. Did the person's physical momentum and accustomed speed of movement and speech seem slowed down?
8. Did the person threaten suicide at any time before actually committing the act?
9. Had the person experienced major losses of dear and intimate persons, or of positions of power and influence, or of positions of respect and esteem before the actual suicide?
10. Does the person have a family history of depression or other forms of mental illness?

If you receive a high percentage of "yes" answers to these ten questions, you can give the family some empirically based assurance that the deceased suffered from one of the most lethal of clinical disorders—depression. We have clinical validation that specific medications actually do correct many biochemical dysfunctions that cause these ten symptoms. With adequate psychotherapy and social readjustment, patients can handle their lives. Considerable numbers of them are restored to the joy of their salvation and to new hope "for the living of these days" by close collaboration between physicians and pastors. Performing the medical or the pastoral task alone is not enough; both must be done simultaneously.

If indeed neither task was performed—as is too often the case, whereupon the suicide becomes an accomplished fact—

then you can answer the family's questions with some degree of precision by using the ten-point inquiry I have suggested above. (Also read Dean Schuyler's *The Depressive Spectrum*, Aronson, 1974, for a thorough, somewhat nontechnical discussion of this whole point of view.)

Here is a second question you may be asked: "Is suicide the unpardonable sin?" This may be sharpened into: "Is my daddy (or my mother, my husband, my wife, as the case may be) in hell?" The question is based on old Catholic and old Protestant assumptions about repentance as a prior necessity for forgiveness. As one person contemplating suicide said to me: "I wish there were a building so tall that I could jump off, repent, and be forgiven before I hit the ground!"

The fallacy in this hyperrational thinking lies in perceiving repentance as a work we perform in order to be forgiven. Grace has a hard time getting through the armor of the "works salvation" of the compulsive, impulse-ridden conscience of persons contemplating suicide. Their unbelief needs help, though they are not devoid of faith in God. The main assurance you and I can give a family about this knotty question is to point out the previous manner of life of the deceased. Often—though certainly not always—they had led exemplary lives for years. By their fruits you can know them —even in a death like this. A single event—tragic in its finality—cannot be the basis of God's care and judgment, because God sees the whole of a person's life and not just the way it ended.

Another assurance that you can give, even to the family of someone whose life was a long series of tragic defeats, is that the corporate community as a whole bears responsibility, not just the deceased and the immediate family. The distribution of responsibility is a pastoral function. All we like sheep have gone astray, but God has intervened in our behalf through Jesus Christ.

Whatever you as a pastor do, I am sure you will not dodge or gloss over this second question. It is one the pastor cannot refer to others. You and I are the last court of appeal for such questions. Let's be sure to take a firm, clear, and yet consoling stand.

Another question you may be asked: "Is this hereditary? Am I in danger of doing the same thing myself?" The matter of the genetic coding of suicide is not an exact science yet. The findings of various studies, including the concurrence of mental disorders in parents and offspring, provide a general kind of evidence that manic-depressive and depressive constitutions are hereditary. However, more recent biochemical discoveries about the role of antidepressants and lithium in the treatment of these disorders have removed some of the fatalism formerly associated with them. Moreover, discoveries of social psychiatry in the demographic or populational studies of depression and suicide have found high correlations between these and oppressive social injustices in the work systems, in the exploitation of trapped and helpless persons, and in the deprivations attendant on crowded living space. The collapse of ordered and secure social systems, such as one finds in some religious groups, tends to increase the incidence of depression and suicide.

Another question you will be asked: "Was this an accident? Did our loved one simply make a mistake in taking medication or in the use of a firearm?"

The actual method used by the suicide is your key to handling this question. For example, one who is accustomed to abusing alcohol can very easily miscalculate the dosage prescribed by the physician. Or the extremely aged person may forget how much medication was taken and when. This kind of disorientation can lead to an unintended overdose. On the other hand, in the case of someone who uses a shotgun and places the muzzle of the gun in his mouth and pulls the trigger, there is little likelihood that death was accidental. Likewise the person who is found in a closed car, with the engine going and a hose running from the exhaust pipe to the interior, must have planned deliberately to die of carbon-monoxide poisoning.

A better approach is ask whether this suicide was deliberate or impulsive. The margin of error and accident is much higher in the latter than in the former. For example, there is the case of a seventy-year-old woman living alone who bolted upright in bed out of her sleep and said to herself: "My God! I am totally alone in the world and no one cares whether I live or die." She leaped from the bed, grabbed a kitchen knife and slashed her wrist and throat badly. As she began to bleed to death, she called her downstairs neighbor, who called an emergency medical team. They rushed her to a hospital, where surgeons saved her life. If she *had* been alone in the world, she would never have called her neighbor. Her mistake was on the side of life, not death.

Contrast this with a man who shot himself through the mouth with a shotgun. The suicide notes indicated that he had been planning the act for months. He even put his family in touch with helping pastors before he did so! This was no accident, nor did he leave room for error in his demise.

The place to deal with these questions is not at the public funeral but in family conference. I have found it helpful to have a series of family conferences with as many members as are available. In this way you can assess who needs what kind of care, and you can gradually develop a community-support system that will bring in others to help sustain the family through the disaster that has befallen them.

The Funeral of a Suicide

A brief introduction of the purpose of the gathering of friends in the community of faith can open the funeral service. I prefer to describe the death of the loved one as sudden, tragic, and beyond the mind of man to grasp at the time. We are gathered to affirm to the family that they are not alone in their grief. Our community of faith in Christ was formed and functions daily to inspire us to bear one another's burdens and so fulfill the law of Christ.

Another purpose is to assure the family that this time of tragedy serves to remind us that we all are repeatedly being tested to determine whether we can open ourselves to the help of others or whether we must keep all matters in our own hands —even the matter of our own death—and try to live and die as self-sufficient persons. Human beings do not really live unto themselves, nor die unto themselves. The presence of family, friends, and fellow Christians demonstrates our quiet confessions that we all deeply need each other and that we do not intend to live shut off from others at a time of great despair.

In the presence of God, a suicide is a death that need not have happened. Our times and our community are thrown out of joint by such a death.

Herein lies purpose and meaning in all this suffering: that we shall all learn something from the one whose self-sacrifice carries a message to us about loneliness and community. That death called for some kind of commitment and resolve. What kind of commitment and resolve about how to live life, and to live it abundantly, does this suggest to each of us? Such pain as this unique grief makes us think and pray; thinking and praying makes us wise; wisdom in the reverence for God makes us strong to bear the misery, the hurt that this tragedy has brought to us all.

I would use Scriptures like Gal. 6:1–10; Rom. 7:18–25; Ps. 13; and Rev. 21:1–4; 22:1–5.

I would suggest building a prayer out of the materials found in Rom. 8:26–27 and I Cor. 10:11–13. I would extend the affection and confidant relationship of the whole congregation in a solemn recommitment to bear unbearable loads together.

Other motifs for funeral planning can be used, but having observed many, many cases of suicide, I am singularly impressed that each person died *alone, all alone.* However, you can find innumerable ways to appeal from that loneliness and impress on the family and the larger audience that community is the purpose of the body of Christ, even in the presence of death.

SOME WAYS OF PREDICTING AND PREVENTING SUICIDE

One can be global and say that positive meaning and purpose in life are inherent in the Christian faith, and that this will anticipate and prevent suicide. Yet this reduces the task to truisms that we all affirm and yet have no specific way to implement. Several guidelines can be given that are specific.

First, you can raise the consciousness of a congregation to be aware of the lethal character of isolation. A small face-to-face company of concerned and committed persons can be a spawning ground for varieties of illnesses, not the least of which is depression. But you can concentrate your leadership's attention on the life-preserving power of a close-knit Sunday school class, a youth group, a choir, an official board. These groups are potential reducers of isolation and key communicators of illness and distress of any kind, particularly with drop outs from community.

Second, the criteria of depression given above can be

taught at the group level. They are no secret, and need no intensive education to be learned. They require accurate empathy, the powers of observation, and the basic gumption and common sense I find in humble but wise people in all stations of life. If as intimate a matter as examination for breast cancer and as difficult a process as coronary pulmonary resuscitation can be taught to hundreds of thousands, then the criteria for identifying genuine depression in oneself and others can be taught, and the last stages of despair can be prevented by early detection and treatment.

Third, in talking with those who actually threaten suicide or express a fear of committing suicide, the myths about the act can be subordinated to the hard facts.

Myth 1. "People who speak aloud of suicide will never do it." Many people who ultimately killed themselves had repeatedly talked of it to others.

Myth 2. "People who threaten suicide are simply attention-getters. Ignore the attention-getting device and they will quit using it." Not so. Suicide actually accomplished is a way of branding oneself into the attention of others.

Myth 3. "If you get them to promise you they will not commit suicide, they will not do it." Not so. The promise may predispose them not to do so, but it cannot be trusted indefinitely. Other measures are necessary.

What multiple measures can be taken?

First, measure the lethality of the threat on the following scale:

1. Has this person ever attempted suicide before? How many times?
2. In the family history, have parents or siblings ever taken their own lives?
3. Has this person ever been acutely depressed, or is there a history of chronic depression?

4. Has this person considered a specific way of committing suicide? Measure the lethality of the means on the following descending scale of gravity:
   a. Guns, particularly handguns.
   b. Hanging, particularly with a rope.
   c. Drowning, particularly if this person cannot swim.
   d. Carbon monoxide from a car exhaust.
   e. Leaping from heights.
   f. Legal drugs, on a scale of known lethality.
   g. Any mixture of legal or illegal drugs with large quantities of alcohol.
   h. Commercial poisons, Drano, lye, and others.
   i. Over-the-counter sleeping medications such as Sominex.
   j. Lethal quantities of alcohol taken rapidly on an empty stomach.
   k. Aspirin, Tylenol, Bufferin, or other pain-reliever taken in large quantities.
5. Has this person been severely depressed and shown a sudden, dramatic improvement and serene happiness? This may indicate a decision to commit suicide and a resolve to put everything in order before doing so.
6. Do friends and relatives have an impression of being told good-by?
7. Has this person complained of being abandoned by God, or the Holy Spirit? (Remarkably enough, I have never heard anyone speak of being forsaken by Jesus.)
8. Is this person afraid of having committed, or being about to commit, "the unpardonable sin"?
9. Does this person think delusionally, assuming the identity of Christ *about to be crucified?*

The following are criteria that I have used clinically and found to be reliable not only in assessing the lethality of the suicidal urge but also as signals for taking several preventive steps:

1. To ask permission to arrange a visit to a physician, possibly this person's family physician, immediately. If there is no family or personal physician, and a psychiatrist is available, I make the referral directly there. However, to have the recommendation come from a known and trusted family physician is best in most cases, though not in all.

2. To alert close relatives and friends to be on guard against possible suicidal actions. (A threat of suicide—or homicide—is *not* private confessional data.) It is best for the troubled individual to do the alerting personally, but if not, I try to do so in a calm and matter-of-fact way. Panic reactions in others may energize the impulse and hasten the act of suicide.

3. If a sleep disorder is present, to do everything possible to have it corrected by medical attention. Add to this your own daily contact by telephone, letter, or visit. It is better to see such a person often but briefly, rather than to spend long hours at one time.

4. To mobilize the support available from relatives, friends, and professional persons. Basic frustrations growing out of work, family, or religious beliefs must be removed at the same time as the medical care is being administered.

5. If need be, to support wholeheartedly a physician's recommendation that this person be hospitalized. Nursing care is one advantage in this move. And removal from the accustomed environment often prevents impaired-judgment decisions that can embarrass, handicap, and hinder the most rapid recovery.

6. If this person is hospitalized, to maintain the prescribed privacy and to encourage congregations to do likewise. Written messages of encouragement to health are better

than large-scale visiting, which should be limited to people who are close to the patient in a positive way. (Of course, this is true of any patient who is seriously ill.)
7. To provide follow-up convalescent care when the patient moves back into society. The book by John Hewett is helpful at this point, too. The data I give here is meant to serve as background for you as pastor. George Bennett's book on the care of mental patients upon their return home is also a real assistance at this stage.

The important purpose underlying this whole chapter is to provide you as a pastor with useful information about depression and suicide. You are a teacher come from God who can provide the hope of the Christian gospel in dealing with the wish and will to live and live abundantly among the extended family of the people of God in Jesus Christ.

Suggestions for Further Reading

Hatton, Corrine Loing; Valente, S. M.; and Rink, Alice. *Suicide: Assessment and Intervention.* Appleton-Century-Crofts, 1977.

Reynolds, David K., and Farberow, Norman L. *Suicide: Inside and Out.* University of California Press, 1976.

Shneidman, Edwin S.; Farberow, Norman L.; and Litman, Robert E. *The Psychology of Suicide.* Science House, 1970.

5. The Pastoral Care of Working Parents

The family in America is undergoing rapid change in lifestyle, child-rearing assumptions, and especially in the situation of women in the work force as well as in the home. In 1958, 9.3 million families were "Two-Breadwinner Marriages." In 1978, 19.4 million families had both husband and wife as breadwinners. ("Two Incomes: No Sure Hedge Against Inflation," *U.S. News & World Report,* July 9, 1979, p. 45.)

What kinds of work are the wives doing? In 1970, the statistics looked like this:

1970

% Distribution for Females (Total U.S.) by Occupation	Labor Force (Age 16 and over)
Professional, technical, and kindred workers (nurses, teachers, technicians, etc.)	15.7%
Managers and administrators	3.6
Sales workers	7.4
Clerical and kindred workers	34.9
Craftsmen, foremen, and kindred workers	1.8
Operatives (except transport)	13.9
Transport equipment operatives	.5
Laborers (except farm)	1.0

Farmers/farm managers	.2
Farm laborers	.5
Service workers (except household)	16.6
Private household workers	3.9

(Characteristics of the Population, U.S. Summary, Vols. 1 and 2, U.S. Government Census 1970.)

Clearly the majority of working women were, in 1970, clustered—even trapped—in nonprofessional jobs rather than careers—84.3 percent. This figure is composed primarily of three groups—clerical workers, factory operatives, and service workers: 65.4 percent. You can readily see that you as a pastor will appreciate the work of Wade and Mary Jo Rowatt on working parents, because a number of them must be among your church members.

How do the problems of working parents come to your attention as a pastor? Only rarely will anyone ask you for a book to read on the subject. When you are asked, however, or when you discern that such problems exist among your people, you have a surprising resource for them in the Rowatts' book in the Westminster Christian Care series.

The Unfulfilled Woman

The first point at which these problems come to your attention is when a mother expresses her confusion about priorities: "Which should I put first, my job, my children, my husband, my own satisfactions?" This question may come up when the church asks her to do something like serving in the vacation church school or helping with the work of the official board.

Back in the late 1940s, after the impact of World War II had caused so many women to enter the work force, several studies of the happiness of professionally trained women suggested a pattern of advice that I have found helpful. If a woman is professionally educated, she tends to feel guilty if she has children and either works full time or spends full time caring for them and doing housework. If she works full time outside the home while her children are less than three years of age, she feels cheated because she cannot enjoy her baby, and guilty for not caring for the baby herself.

On the other hand, if she stays at home full time, she feels that she is losing touch with other adults, and is left out of the action world of adults.

Therefore, if such a mother can work *part time* when she has children under the age of three, she tends to feel much happier with life. But the scarcity of part-time jobs is a very great problem in itself. Consequently, writers in today's women's-movement literature make a very legitimate appeal for part-time work.

The Reentering Woman

The second point at which you will encounter the problems of working parents comes when a mother whose children are already in school wants to reenter the work force after having spent several years as a full-time housewife. She is likely to express regret that she did not get her graduate degree earlier, to qualify as a full-fledged professional. She may be restless, anxious, and mixed in her emotions. Is life passing her by? Her complaints about her husband are usually vague, but the most persistent one is that he doesn't seem to understand why she is upset. After all, is he not providing for her well? Why does she want to work if they don't need the money? What he does not appreciate is that she needs a meaningful identity of her own apart from his.

If this is the core problem, then an interview with both the wife and the husband may help them to communicate and develop a plan to fulfill the woman's more spiritual needs in some appropriate form of work.

THE CONJOINT SEARCH FOR WORK

Another point of contact with the problems of working parents comes when a couple are seeking placement after graduation from school—whether in law, medicine, theology, art, social work, or business. This critical occasion raises the question of whose vocational needs shall take precedence over the other's. The competitive-cooperative pendulum moves back and forth in your interviews with them. They need candor and considerateness in a fine blend at this time. Your own assumptions will be tested: Do you think the man's employment should take precedence as a matter of course? Are the needs of both of equal importance by definition? How can an effective balance of these be worked out?

In this kind of situation, a couple's having actual offers of positions gives concreteness to the discussion. Their thinking is much less abstract when specific offers are being considered. You can be helpful as a person who stays in touch with openings in their field, as a person who can refer or introduce them to potential employers, and as one who can write letters of recommendation. A sustaining relationship with you lessens their sense of isolation and their anxiety over the unknown that lies ahead of them.

THE LOSS OF A JOB

Another time of concern for working parents is at the point of job loss or job change. If the wife retains her job and the husband loses his, then she becomes the sole source of economic support until he finds another job. If their relationship is strong and healthy, the strain is heavy but manageable. Your knowledge of their past history helps you to assess the threat to the marriage itself. You, in any case, wait with them during the long process of preparing résumés, arranging interviews; waiting for replies to applications.

In this situation, the historical assumption that husbands are measured by their ability to earn money presents the man with an ego-strength crisis of full magnitude. However, this is where the teaching that the true liberation of women is a liberation of men as well—a teaching I genuinely believe to be true—comes into prominent view. A marriage today is at risk when only one member has enough marketable skills to provide for the family. Similarly, the family is at risk when only one member knows how to prepare meals, shop for daily necessities, keep children clean and happily occupied, and balance the family checkbook. The modern home is much like a small Navy combat ship—every crew member must know every other crew member's skill, so that in case one member is wounded or dies or deserts ship, others can cover his duties. Furthermore, in such a joint knowledge of skills, the person who happens to be closest at the time can do what is necessary. The Rowatts demonstrate this sharing of skills all through their book.

Sources of Emotional Support

Collean and Frank Johnson present a study of twenty-eight two-career families. All had at least one child under the age of twelve. The mean age of all the children was 5.6. These parents tended to "tighten the boundaries around the nuclear family" and to choose their friends among other two-career families rather than turn to their own parental-grandparental families. (Collean Leahy Johnson, and Frank A. Johnson,

"Attitudes Toward Parenting in Dual-Career Families," *American Journal of Psychiatry,* pp. 391–395, Vol. 134, No. 4, April 1977.)

Middle-class two-career families such as were studied by Johnson and Johnson find common cause with other middle-class career families. They all tend to have much in common during the years of professional training and during their so-called starvation period of becoming established in their professional careers. However, the professions are not alike in pay and prestige. In time the persons involved go into the high-pay and high-prestige professions of medicine, law, and business on the one hand, and others go into teaching, social work, nursing, and psychology on the other hand. Yet all these professions have one circumstance in common, that their work does not leave neatly demarcated times for rest, recreation, family rituals, and communication. As a result, these professionals are more likely to internalize their work, and this creates separate worlds for husbands and wives in the same family but different professions.

One of the creative ministries you as a pastor can perform, therefore, is to concentrate on getting persons of different professions to know each other in the context of the life of the church. Far too many professional persons of all ages whom I know feel like by-standers—kibitzing what is happening. The church can be a wider family of support for these persons by getting them acquainted with each other and by giving their talents expression in the ongoing life of genuinely belonging to the church.

Do-It-Yourself Work

Dual-career spouses are often products of ambitious blue-collar homes. Their parents scrimped and saved to give them "a better life," placing much confidence in education—

though fathers and mothers were not always in agreement on the worth of schooling. Nevertheless, in the earliest years of "getting a start" in their careers, dual-career persons use their earlier blue-collar family skills. They remodel their own houses, plant gardens, barter skills with each other. One who is adept at electrical work will swap time with a person who grew up helping his parents in a garden. The one helps install a lighting system; the other repays by helping plan and plant a garden.

One major problem brought to you as a pastor by working parents is their inability to control adolescent sons or daughters. In a sense, the parents are ten years too late in formulating the problem. They neglected to pass their own hand-oriented skills on to their sons and daughters. Now "keeping them off the streets," and making them "come in on time" at night, is the cry for help. Much of this can be prevented if the skills of working with one's hands were either bequeathed as a heritage or learned through a hobby in the years from age six to thirteen and developed to the point of earning money in the years thirteen to sixteen. The professional couple need not be too surprised, however, if at least one of their offspring chooses a blue-collar lifework rather than one of the high-discipline professions. Nor should they be surprised if that son or daughter earns more money than the poorly paid teacher, psychologist, minister, or social worker.

Interaction with the Opposite Sex

The entry, exit, and reentry of women into the work arena of the middle classes poses the problem of husbands' and wives' responsible interaction with persons of their opposite sex on the job. If the husband and wife team wittingly or unintentionally have neglected to communicate with each other over a considerable length of time, it is only natural that their relationships to others in the work arena will come to mean more and more. Purely professional relationships with someone of the opposite sex may become tinged at first with emotional dependence. If the relationship is allowed to extend beyond the restriction of the job to long lunches, to shared evening work or business trips, then the dependence takes on a more complete involvement with or without sexual complications. Many affairs and clandestine liaisons are gradually formed in this way.

Yet to say "Tut, tut; these things are awful and should not be" tends both to make them worse and to avoid the problem they present to Christians. I say Christians because the work arena can be the church staff members as we interact with each other and with active church members. The critical question is: "What is the creative place for persons of the opposite sex in the lives of Christian husbands and wives?"

The First Letter to Timothy deals with this in part (I Tim. 5:1–2): "Do not rebuke an older man but exhort him as you would a father; treat younger men like brothers, older women like mothers, younger women like sisters, in all purity."

However, such familial bonds may be annoying and confusing to colleagues of the opposite sex. They may feel that they are being diminished to be seen as fathers, brothers, mothers, and sisters, and not as colleagues. Yet these words of I Timothy cannot be laid aside so easily; the psychodynamics of human relationships are woven according to these basic patterns mentioned in the Scripture. For example, a co-worker may indeed be the brother a woman never had, the sister a man lost to leukemia early in his life, the father he never knew or the mother he wishes his own mother had been like. Therefore, these basic transferences and deprivations need to be examined closely, either through personal reflection or counseling or, preferably, both.

In the meantime, the important thing to rely upon in such

relationships is the additional value that becoming a professional has added to our distinctly Christian experience—the value of professional competence. Treating our colleagues of the opposite sex as competent colleagues is the primary conscience factor in relating ourselves to them. Undergirding this professional criterion is our faith in God as the Creator of them in his image and our faith in Christ who died for them as a person. Treating a colleague as someone of competence and not as a wailing wall for our timidity and lack of candor with our spouse is the essence of positive regard and rewarding satisfaction. To do otherwise is both to sin as a Christian and to breach professional ethics as a colleague.

I am conversant with the concept of open marriage, in which sexual liaisons outside of wedlock are looked upon as the right of enlightened spouses. I am also aware of the element of greed for money, position, and power scrambled into the seemingly casual sexual relationships among business, professional, and even ecclesiastical leaders. The multiplex of motives is not a simple ABC sexual involvement. The major imperative remains: true professionals are bound—whether they accept it or not—by the need to face honestly and openly their own marriage relationship's demands and offers of comfort before the formation of even a dependency on someone else is allowed. To do less than this is to do violence to more than one's spouse; it is by act or word to do equal harm to the other member of the opposite sex as well.

Furthermore, "sticking to business" is the prudential ethical precept that keeps one's relationship to a person of the opposite sex in clear focus. The reward for this is the dignity, respect, and trust of all the staff members of the opposite sex rather than the private adulation of one who knows that both of you are fudging on integrity and fair play. All this may seem afield from the theme of working parents and their relationship to their children. It is not. Suffice it to say that children are the ultimate concern in these matters. Will you as pastor sense these concerns of working parents?

BLUE-COLLAR WORKING PARENTS

Not all working parents are of the middle class. Yet many middle-class persons become part of two-career families if one defines a career as a position achieved after many years of educational preparation. Also, the low-prestige professions have much in common with the most advantageously employed blue-collar workers. The latter usually have a high school education or less. The husband-wife pair both work. She works, often not by choice but by necessity. The husband may be a delivery man, a postal clerk, a night watchman, a miner, a weaver, a truck driver. The wife may work at a factory inspecting light bulbs, as an anonymous typist in an office pool, as a salesperson or checkout clerk in a department store. She does these repetitive tasks because she and her husband need her wages to pay their bills. If they are lucky, there is a grandmother, aunt, or cousin to take care of the children during working hours.

The husband ordinarily does not take part in the care of the home and the children. That is woman's work. The home is the only place where he can exercise authority. This "Archie Bunker" attitude toward women and the home is a painful example of a man's effort to maintain leadership of the family.

You as a pastor are most likely to see this tension when a young person, a late adolescent son or daughter of one of these homes, comes to church. The parents may or may not do so. (After all, it costs money to go to church. They say that is what pastors want most anyhow!) But young persons can "ride free." In the process, their eagerness to go to college becomes a strong desire. The church helps them to contact college authorities. A bright mind, eager to learn, wins the cooperation of the school. But—the father objects: "The kid already has more education than common sense." How can you help the young person to push ahead, knowing that the father senses that all that learning will make his own son or daughter a stranger to him? All the while, the mother may be taking on more work so that her child will have a good education and have a life that is better than hers.

If you are a pastor in an industrial community, you can supply many cases to illustrate my last paragraph. As Lillian Rubin says: "But few working-class wives are free to make the choice about working inside or outside the home depending on only their own desires. Most often, economic pressures dictate what they will do, and *even those who wish least to work outside the home probably will do so sometimes in their lives.*" (Lillian Rubin, *Worlds of Pain: Life in the Working Class Family,* p. 168; Basic Books, 1976.)

For families like these, the church itself can become a form of continuing the education of people in their weekday free time. Having a class in Bible coupled with a frank emphasis on learning to read better—increasing one's vocabulary, pronouncing words correctly, getting verbs and subjects to agree, and so on—would not appeal to many at first. If the fathers can be made comfortable doing this, a sociological miracle will have just occurred! Why not try it?

Blue-collar parents' work, like the work of other classes, actually sets the stage for marital conflict. Separate shifts, separate duties, long hours in overtime, or moonlighting on second jobs result in the same stresses of exposure to fellow workers of the opposite sex. Among blue-collar couples, violence in marital conflict more often takes the form of physical abuse due to alcoholism than in the middle classes. However, the psychological violence of the middle classes, even in the misuse of religion, can be more mystifying sadistic.

The best preventive approach to problems in the work arena I have found is suggested by Harry Haskell Rightor in his book *Pastoral Counseling in Work Crises* (Judson Press, 1979). He rightly says that the pastor is the "last of the generalists" available to a great many people. He writes both to you and your lay leadership in an effort to encourage both you and them to recognize and deal with work crises throughout your congregation.

The problems of working parents point up many issues of social justice in your pastoral world. Are women at work being used by industry, business, and institutions to justify low pay of the men to whom they are married? Does the mother of children have a chance in her exits and reentries into the work force? To what extent does conspicuous consumerism beguile both parents into living beyond their means, thus putting things ahead of humans, including themselves and their own happiness and health?

Credit buying is a money problem encouraged in the exorbitant building of churches as well as in the working parents who buy on the installment plan—at 12 percent to 18 percent a year. (I hesitate to put these figures down; they may be too small by the time this book is published.) Again, are women simply an auxiliary work force while we wait for another war to kill their children?

The systems of business, industry, schools, hospitals, etc., that employ persons need large populations of workers—both "staff" and "employees" who are willing to "stay put" without advancement beyond partial cost-of-living raises. The systems call for snuffing out the need to grow. Are the systems' decision makers members of a church? It is to their social advantage to be members. What are the claims of a gospel of justice, mercy, and humility in all these and many more situations? How is the love of God and neighbor made known here?

Suggestions for Further Reading

Bolles, Richard N. *The Three Boxes of Life: And How to Get Out of Them.* Ten Speed Press, 1978.

Coles, Robert. *Migrants, Mountaineers and Sharecroppers.* Atlantic Monthly Press, 1971.

Work in America, Report of a Special Task Force to the Secretary of Health, Education, and Welfare. MIT Press, 1973.

Warner, W. Lloyd. *Social Class in America.* Harper & Row, 1960. Paperback.

6. Pastoral Care as the Discipline of Character

Paul Schmidt writes as a psychologist who is Christian. Therefore, he takes the demands of Christian character development seriously. Both he and I are alarmed by the widespread tendency of Christians and non-Christians alike to consider every human problem—even death—as a disease that can be cured.

Formerly, problems of family strife, job dissatisfaction and insecurity, delinquent behavior, and lack of integrity in human beings were never regarded as diseases. However, the sense of personal responsibility for one's own behavior has withered. In its place has grown the idea that all human frailty is a disease. Its cure lies outside the person, in the efficacy of a therapy that others sell. Little wonder that, for many, the cause lies outside the person too—in parents, teachers, the Establishment, demons, evil spirits, the devil, or the stars!

I write this chapter assuming that some disorders of human personality do derive from biochemical imbalances of the body, but that few forms of human misbehavior can be treated by medical means. They are disorders of human character, reflecting the absence, breakdown, or shirking of people's sense of personal responsibility for their lives. Therefore, to be healthy in this way is not a right but a personal moral obligation.

You as a pastor will see this absence, breakdown, or shirking of responsibility in individuals and in the family setting as well. The demands of seeing adolescents through their storms and stresses are great. They fall upon both the adolescents and their parents. It is easy for a son or daughter, on the one hand, or the mother or father, on the other, to "cut and run" in the face of these demands. These crises of character have background, can be understood, even predicted. Yet understanding is no substitute for courage and commitment on the part of parents and children.

The home is one crucible of character formation. The school is another. The church is still another. The freely chosen peer group is yet one more. One school of thought, missing both the independent existence of these forces and the interplay between them, blames all character disorders on one or another crucible: the home, the school, the church, or the peer group. None of these is to blame, but all are responsible.

You as a pastor have families come to you about one of their children. They say: "How can one person cause so much trouble?" You have heard public school teachers or church school teachers ask about a given boy or girl: "What kind of home can this young person come from? Surely it must be a very unhappy one." Sometimes both public school and church school teachers joining forces with the parents say: "Can't you talk with this child and put an end to such behavior?" The family may be one of the finest Christian families, but this one member is a black sheep, an embarrassment to all the rest.

Some examples of this kind of person are:
— Reckless drivers—youths who speed or who drive while intoxicated with alcohol or other perception-disturbing substances.

— Persons who are unwilling to work either on a money-earning job or on academic studies.
— Persons who squander or misuse family money, i.e., always "being broke," living beyond their personal income.
— Persons who steal, such as shoplifters or burglars.
— Persons who are sexual deviants, such as exhibitionists, molesters, rapists, and pseudohomosexuals.
— Persons who run away from home, going on wanderlust trips, taking up with gypsylike groups of peers who drift from place to place.
— Persons who are sexually promiscuous, with attendant contraction of venereal disease, or repeated pregnancy and demands for abortions.
— Persons who blindly attach themselves to an authoritarian group that demands total loyalty to the exclusion of parents, siblings, school, and church. These groups are often small communes with no public visibility or name. Sometimes they become front-page names, such as the Unification Church and the Peoples Temple.
— Persons who marry and divorce many times, and depend inordinantly on grandparents to supply stability in the lives of any children.
— Authoritarian religious leaders who command large followings, who fleece them for money, who spend at a garish and ostentatious pace without accounting to anyone.
— Denominational and secular power tycoons who control rubber-stamp official boards. They create a bureaucratic system that punishes anyone who complains about the lack of due process in decision-making. Their financial and legal behavior is beyond public scrutiny. To some they dispense blandishments in the form of

sentimental catch phrases, yet they are brutal in their punishment of dissidents in their organization.

These persons are spoken of in the technical literature as "antisocial" or "sociopathic" personalities. Paul Schmidt gives a very detailed picture of various patterns of behavior found in a wide spectrum of such personalities. Those who work in psychiatry tend to dismiss any of these persons who occasionally get into a program of psychiatric treatment. They enroll mainly because they are driven by social or legal pressures, such as expulsion from school, the loss of a job, threats of divorce by a mate, actual punishment after having been convicted of a felony such as stealing, passing bad checks, embezzlement, sexual molestation of children, exhibitionism, and so on.

Such sociopaths become "authoritarian referrals"; they are there because of external pressure, not from personal choice. They feel they have been sentenced to psychiatric treatment, so treatment time becomes "serving" time. The critical point of psychiatric treatment, then, lies in the skill of the physician to transform the patient's motivation from an external one to one that is internal and personally chosen.

You as a pastor have the same problem when you visit such a person uninvited or when, let us say, a husband or wife or an adolescent is sent to you by a spouse or a parent. For example, an adolescent boy who has come home drunk twice in one week may be "grounded" by his parents. This is very wise. However, having the son (or a daughter) come to you as pastor for counseling as a means of being "ungrounded" is quite another thing. It is unwise. You are about to be used as an escape device for the adolescent. Frank confrontation of this matter on the first conversation with both the parent and the adolescent is necessary. Reject that kind of covenant outright. Just resisting it will teach far more than ten interviews—nine of which may be wasted.

Already we have entered the arena of the "power politics" played by the family in caring for someone who seeks emotional release in drunkenness and other kinds of antisocial behavior. Before we go further, however, I think it wise to identify the recurrent characteristics of those who have become habitually antisocial. The following checklist will help you to assess more precisely the person at hand:

A Behavior Profile of the Antisocial Personality

1. Does this person have a superficial charm, make a flashy first impression, rely on good looks and glibness to "con" you with compliments?
2. Does this person have a self-image of cleverness, believing that others are stupid?
3. Is this person unreliable in keeping promises, carrying out assignments, maintaining contact with you even when not in trouble or in need of something?
4. Have there been occasions when this person has used you, your name, or your property?
5. Do you find this person being repeatedly untruthful even while maintaining a veneer of sincerity?
6. Does this person repeatedly show poor judgment and fail to learn from past mistakes or to profit from experience?
7. Is this person apt to be exceptionally self-centered, lacking in empathy, or unable to establish and maintain lasting relationships, especially with persons of the opposite sex?
8. Does this person seem devoid of any sense of personal guilt about acts committed?
9. Does this person show exceptional indifference to moral responsibilities, emotional appeals for fair play, and the hurt feelings of others?

10. Is this person casual, trivial, superficial, and even imper-
sonal about sexual relationships?

11. Is this person given to mushily sweet sentimentality?
I am indebted to H. M. Cleckley, in his book *The Mask
of Sanity*, 4th ed. (C. V. Mosby, 1964), for some of the
above formulations. This book remains one of the defini-
tive treatises on the subject of the antisocial, or sociopathic,
or psychopathic personality—the three terms used to refer
to the person who acts out inner conflicts, externalizing the
problem and imposing it on everyone nearby.

SOME WORKING HYPOTHESES AND CORRESPONDING PATTERNS OF PASTORAL APPROACH

You are puzzled and mystified by these persons. You search
for a way of being an effective pastor to them without being
engulfed by the uproar they create. They seem to keep those
around them in perpetual turmoil, including you as a pastor.
What are the meanings of their behavior and, on the basis of
those meanings, what can you do and refuse to do that might
engender in these persons a will to learn, change, and grow?

Impaired Ability to Attach

Bonds are formed between mother and infant. John
Bowlby calls this "attachment." If the bond of attachment is
broken, he says, the child goes through three stages: protest,
despair, and apathy. Then a new attachment is formed, to a
mother substitute. If this bond is allowed to remain, grow,
and be enriched, the child is not at risk. Yet if that and
succeeding bondings are broken, the child sooner or later
ceases to form attachments, perceiving such commitments as
ultimately painful. As an adult, then, the grown child is an
affable, superficial, uncommitted individual who does not
form durable relationships because the basic trust of the in-

fant has been repeatedly quelled into a basic distrust. The person will habitually reenact situations that prove this attitude to be right—that people cannot be trusted.

Consequently, the long-term testing of your own and your church's trustworthiness, even to "tell it like it is" when your trust in such a person has been shaken, is the primary principle of pastoral care. Your first impulse, for example, is to go "all out" to prove that you are loving, generous, and caring; but then you are heading toward a big disappointment when this person concludes that you are "just like all the rest of them." It would be better to lay this primary principle on the table right at the outset, to declare that the two of you are testing each other's trustworthiness. Trust cannot be built overnight, but it does grow through testing. Is your counselee willing to join with you in Experiment Trust and see how you get along?

Such people have learned to do unto others as others (they believe) have done unto them. Are they now willing to start learning to do unto others as the others would have done unto them? This summary of the Law and the Prophets (Matt. 7:12) is the beginning of the conversion, especially if we see conversion as a "turning around" in one's faith in others, in oneself, and in God.

This is not a bootstrap operation. Neither is it a quick, magical solution. It is a discipline that both you and your counselee can learn together. The first test will be whether or not you find a true desire to continue your discussions about shaken and reestablished trust. This issue can be defined and illustrated face to face during your first interview. (For further study of the problem, see Erik Erikson's "The Golden Rule in the Light of New Insight," *Insight and Responsibility*, p. 231; W. W. Norton & Co., 1964. Also, John Bowlby, *Attachment and Loss*, pp. 27ff.; Vol. I of *Attachment;* Basic Books, 1969.)

The primary goal of your pastoral relationship is to develop mutuality between this person and the Christian fellowship. The Golden Rule makes good sense; you can use it to appeal to the person's cleverness. The Golden Rule also implies sympathetic imagination, because by grace you can hope to cause "chords that were broken to vibrate once more." Yet both good sense and sympathy, with an easygoing reciprocity, are yours to share.

Divide and Conquer the Inconsistent

Another widely agreed upon understanding of the antisocial personality pattern is that the uproar it causes grows out of inconsistent parental guidance. If one parent, for example, is extremely harsh, the other may compensate by being overprotective and indulgent. Or the same parent may alternate between being harsh and punitive, at one time, and exceptionally soft, indulgent, and oversentimental at other times. In either case, the growing child learns early to survive by playing one side against the other. The parents have not disciplined themselves to be consistent, and the child takes advantage of the inconsistency to do as he or she pleases and to get what he or she wants.

You will observe that your church will tend to be divided on how to deal with this person. The strict "law and order" types will be in contention with the permissive "love them into righteousness" types. You yourself may be indecisive as a result. This "acting out" person does not need harsh law and order, sentimentalism, or indecision, but someone who will be consistent, whose yes is yes and no is no (anything more than this comes from evil—Matt. 5:37).

Once again you find your own integrity being tested as you move between the Scylla and Charybdis of law and grace. You do not reward this person's instinctive ploy to "divide and conquer." You set limits to what you can and will do and establish some degree of consistency by benignly neglecting to become upset, be "conned," or be manipulated. You maintain a cool-handed friendship. You do not lend money, arrange to have traffic tickets canceled, or cosign notes at the bank for this person. When you are asked, "Why not?" you reply that you never do such favors for anyone and will not make an exception now.

Your church members say: "But that fine young person will have to stay in that dirty old jail. Aren't you ashamed of yourself?" You say: "No, I can't say that I am. You may be the victim in this person's next collision, and I wouldn't want either of you to be killed. I don't mind visiting in that jail, but I won't arrange a release from it."

Your main frustration, however, is that some trusting soul will indeed arrange a release and pose as a champion for a while. Then the same thing happens again because this person had the God-given right to learn from one's own mistakes taken away by well-meaning but not-so-wise persons. Consistency may, as Emerson said, be foolish. It may be "the hobgoblin of little minds," and "a great soul has simply nothing to do" with it (essay on Self Reliance). However, you are not dealing here with a great soul but with a little mind in the person of a disordered character. We as pastors are so unworldly that the pattern of thinking of the average "con" man or "seductive" woman is foreign to many of us. We propose to be empathic, but if we are to be accurately empathic with persons of disordered character, we learn to cultivate consistency. We let our yes be yes and our no, no.

The Failure of Competence and Fidelity

Another view of the character disorder takes Erik Erikson's ethical development approach seriously. In the grammar grades, the child develops an inferiority feeling about work and follows this up in adolescence by failing to learn the ethical strength of fidelity. Erikson says that the central ethical values of competence in grade school and fidelity in high school do not develop. Instead, a sense of inferiority and uncommittedness emerges, leaving the youngster without a known sense of personal competence or a set of personal loyalties.

These values can be instilled and nurtured in some very practical ways. The school systems, however, aid and abet the sense of personal incompetence by teaching persons that, out of a class of a certain size, a certain percentage have to be failures. The overemphasis on verbal skills neglects the artistic, mechanical, musical, and other nonverbal skills a student may have. But your church need not follow the public schools in this. You can focus on the real strengths and capacities of those who may be adjudged slow in public school. One young person may well be accomplished in music and able to excel in the relatively noncompetitive work of a church's singing groups. Another with artistic skills can employ them in making posters. Whereas instructors can flunk them, or even make fun of them, in a public school or university, a leader in the church can inculcate loyalty in a quiet and unassuming manner.

The matters of competence and loyalty can be topics for discussion in conferences with young persons, or made the subjects of sermons. They can also be means of interpretation to parents who perceive their offspring in totally negative terms.

In the dramas of redemption, competency before God and loyalty to God overcome the time-space problem. The development of one's gifts before God inspires a positive sense of responsibility. The development of loyalty to Jesus Christ transcends the external loyalties to individuals in time and space only.

Work-Study

One of the good results of the Great Depression was that persons attending college had to have jobs in order to make a living. The schools of the era saw to it that much of this work would be educationally relevant. For example, one student would be taught how to grade papers and to assist in the teaching process in other ways. Another would take a job requiring the use certain farm and industrial machinery. One of the great needs today is the kind of education that is basically classical but also diverts some of the exorbitant amounts of play time to useful work in the schools themselves, in the hospitals and health-delivery systems of the community, and in the industrial and business world around the school. This is a systemic rather than a symptom-deploring and symptom-removing treatment of some of the character disorders we see, especially in the more affluent classes of people to whom we minister.

Grandiosity and the Act of Surrender

Harry M. Tiebout, M.D., has made an important contribution to our understanding of and relating to persons with character disorders, especially alcoholics. He says that alcohol addicts ultimately come to a crashing sense of despair; they hit bottom. They cease to deny their plight, give up the sense of all-powerfulness, and admit powerlessness. The key to their surrender is giving up and giving in on the matter of power. (Harry M. Tiebout, "Surrender vs. Compliance in Therapy," *Pastoral Psychology.* Vol. 9, No. 33, April 1958, p. 30.) For persons who are not alcoholics this is a prime spiritual concern —power; but alcoholics control the whole environment they occupy with the behaviors of intoxication.

Similarly, power is the name of the way of life of the ambition-ridden ecclesiastical or governmental demagogues, or the business tycoons, who ruthlessly subject all other interests to their own ends. Do these persons ever hit bottom with their power intoxication? Do they become depressed? Yes. They do so when they are caught in wrongdoing and convicted, or when they are totally frustrated in their ambitions.

Charles Colson describes Haldeman's reaction when Colson suggested that President Nixon should hire a criminal lawyer to ferret out all the facts on Watergate, the hard facts, and "get rid of the culprits": "Just then the phone rang and as Haldeman jerked the receiver towards him, he missed his ear and cracked the hard plastic against his forehead. It was the action of a man under tremendous pressure. *He's powerless,* I suddenly thought, *right in the midst of all this power.*" (Italics author's.) (Charles Colson, *Born Again,* p. 94; Fleming H. Revell Co., 1976.) The rest of the story is about Colson's struggle with the total frustration of his own cleverness and power, which led to his act of surrender and spiritual conversion. He speaks of being challenged by a friend, who handed him C. S. Lewis' book *Mere Christianity.* He sums up the tragic happenings in the White House by quoting Lewis: "Pride is spiritual cancer; it eats up the very possibility of love, or contentment, or even common sense" (*ibid.,* p. 113). He says he felt the way people are said to feel just before death—all the events of his life paraded through his memory. He calls Lewis' words a torpedo that hit him "amidships." Later, after he had left his friend's house, he stopped his car on a lonely dark road and prayed his first real prayer: "God, I don't know how to find you, but I'm going to try! I'm not much the way I am now, but I want to give myself to You!" He repeated the words "Take me" over and over again. He says that "for the first time in my life I was not alone at all" (*ibid.,* p. 117).

You and I as pastors have tended to "program" religious commitment, whether through ecclesiastical ritual, psychological searching for an ultimate cause, or propagandistic showmanship. Consider the plight and possibilities of those who have really hit bottom and are alone in this world. For them, real personal change is at hand.

Persons with severe character disorders are imprisoned, or treated as psychiatric patients to modify the way they behave. Yet only occasionally are they subjected to ethical and spiritual confrontation, and to a forthright challenge of their basic lack of commitment to anyone but themselves. John C. Hoffman rightly says that ethical and spiritual confrontation can be challenging without being moralistic. The resources of fellowship with Christ can be offered to fellow sinners without rebuking them. (John C. Hoffman, *Ethical Confrontation in Counseling,* pp. 88–89; University of Chicago Press, 1979.) Falling into step with them as fellow sinners in a search for the gift of redemption and companionship in Jesus Christ is not the private privilege of a pastor. Others can and do exercise this ministry. However, it is a responsibility, and we are the poorer if we fail to articulate it. We simply join the morally insensitive in their fretful frustrations. The act of surrender is going on all around us—the surrender to a life-long repetition of the same moral blunders, the surrender to the dimmed awareness of alcoholism, drugs, and sexual escapades, the surrender to despair, and the surrender to suicide. I am suggesting that you and I as pastors not be hesitant to make both the offers and expectations of Jesus Christ clear to these persons when they hit bottom.

You as a pastor will see the need for ethical confrontation most often in marriage-counseling situations. Many of them revolve around the hardness of heart of a spouse who knowingly pursues an extramarital affair to the detriment of two families and several working careers. On the part of the innocent spouse, a hardhearted unforgiveness often matches the intransigence of the adulterous one. The Seventh Command-

ment then is used both as excuse and condemnation, and
Jesus' teaching about hardness of heart, or unteachableness,
is ignored. Without rebuke, you can focus on this neglected
spiritual concern without apology and without being a pious
humbug yourself. You can even pray for teachableness yourself! (Pray for me at the same time. In this, we all have gone
astray.)

The Work World and Character Disorders

Alfred Adler often spoke of the "pampered child" syndrome, in which the growing person is actually imbued with
a weakness of spirit by being denied the right of exerting
initiative. A "can't do" or "I don't have to do" way of life is
the result. One of the vicious phenomena of life today is the
lack of skills in two groups of people—the poverty-ridden and
the middle-class affluent youth. One has no opportunity to
work and the other has no need to.

The poor may belong to the second, third, or even fourth
generation to reach the legal age of eighteen with no father
or mother holding a job. Their parents are unemployed or on
welfare, or both. Both parent and growing child are caught
in a trap that is hard to escape from.

The affluent family's sons and daughters have a different
reason for not learning to work: their parents work in a world
separate from the suburbs where they live. All the needs of
the family for both goods and services are bought with money.
Sons and daughters have only vague ideas about the sources
of that money. They are urged to make good grades in school
so as to become professional people or get good jobs. The
parents themselves may be professional people or have good
jobs, but they may be so boxed in by their occupations that
their sons and daughters decide to reject their way of life. The
sons and daughters are also boxed in—at school. And the

grandparents may be boxed in by another circumstance—retirement. Boredom with school, fatigue from overwork, and purposelessness in too much retirement leisure, says Richard N. Bolles, are the "three boxes of life." He proposes that we schedule some education, some work, and some leisure in all three of these stages: youth, adulthood, and later maturity. (Richard N. Bolles, *The Three Boxes of Life: And How to Get Out of Them,* pp. 53–57; Ten Speed Press, 1978.)

The educational system itself aids and abets the insulation of youth from the working world. Mass education too often assumes that somebody must fail if a school is to be regarded as good. (See William Glasser's *Schools Without Failure,* pp. 186–192; Harper & Row, 1969.) Built-in inferiority of a certain percentage of the students is assumed in much computerized test-making and test-taking. A dishonesty or learning for test purposes only is a part of education in character disorder. Yet the most serious deficiency of schools is the demeaning of children whose talents are nonverbal, artistic, or manual in nature. There is a lack of work-study, earn-and-learn programs that include skilled labor in the curricula of even the most affluent as well as of the poverty-stricken. A broader system of rewards is needed, one that includes approbation for others besides the verbally intelligent.

The church programs that heavily accent recreation to the neglect of creative work-achievement programs simply encourage the pathology of families who have enough money to support a church. The development of learning-earning-playing projects would hasten the elimination of the "three boxes of life," and would capture budding young sociopaths before it is too late. After all, pushing drugs is a popular source of income even in elementary-age groups.

You as a pastor may ask now: "Why all this emphasis on the school system and its superficial approaches to youth?

Why all the emphasis on 'work-skill development' in the churches?" Good questions!

The reason is twofold.

First, take a look at the criteria for diagnosing a person as an antisocial personality, and note how success at work is missing in all of them:

1. School problems as manifested by any of the following: truancy, suspension, expulsion, or fighting that leads to trouble with teachers or principals.
2. Staying away from home overnight while living with parents.
3. Troubles with the police of one kind or another.
4. Poor work history as manifested by being fired, quitting without another job to go to, or frequent job changes not accounted for by normal seasonal or economic fluctuations.
5. Marital difficulties as manifested by any of the following: deserting family, two or more divorces, frequent separations due to marital discord, recurrent infidelity, recurrent physical attacks upon spouse, or being suspected of battering a child.
6. Repeated outbursts of rage or fighting not on the school premises.
7. Sexual problems as manifested by any of the following: prostitution, pimping, more than one episode of venereal disease, or flagrant promiscuity.
8. Vagrancy or wanderlust.
9. Persistent and repeated lying or use of an alias.

(See Matti Virkkunen, "Self-Mutilation in Antisocial Personality (Disorder)," *Acta Psychiatrica Scandinavia,* Vol. 54, No. 5, November 1976, p. 348.)

These criteria show clearly that the earliest emergence of a character disorder occurs in school problems, running away from home, truancy, and so on. As the person grows older, the disturbance of the work routine appears in the loss of jobs and the inability to relate effectively to those in authority in the work arena. In adulthood, the disorder manifests itself in the marriage and family life of the person. Running through all the stages is the inability to form and maintain durable relationships with others. And here in America the complications caused by alcohol and drugs appear with distressing regularity.

You as a pastor may look to psychiatry as a panacea for this kind of disordered character. The psychiatrist's success with treatment is probably no better or worse than your own. Many psychiatrists do not perceive these persons as being sick in a classical sense. Others will deal with them forthrightly in a moral and ethical confrontation. Long-term institutional treatment tends to come only after a conviction and imprisonment for a felony. However, the availability of adequate psychiatric attention at this time is difficult to find.

You as a pastor, therefore, will do well to convene an interdisciplinary panel from psychology, social work, public education, psychiatry, and law enforcement. Create a workshop-seminar in which you and they develop your own strategy for dealing with this particular kind of personality disorder. The church is the appropriate community agency to catalyze such a strategy to combat this recurrent problem, which vexes professional persons everywhere.

Your pastoral wisdom will keep you from trying to be the single-handed rescuer of these disordered persons. On the other hand, your same pastoral wisdom will not look to other professional persons as having the final remedy for one who lacks stability of character. Paul Schmidt's book can be of great assistance to you in counseling with the families of such persons, because through it you can put them into a learning frame rather than a blaming frame. Similarly, self-help groups, such as Alcoholics Anonymous, Gamblers Anonymous, and Parents Anonymous (for child abusers and molest-

ers), have had exceptional results in creating a new community and a pattern of steady and caring confrontation for
those who need it. You can learn from these groups principles
that can be modified and adopted by church-sponsored
groups.

As a theologian, you will raise many questions about the
persons who live character-disordered lives. How is it that
their early religious training had no effect? To what extent
should radical evangelical conversion be sought for them?
How is it that their conversions are short-lived in their ethical
and spiritual fruits? To what extent is a special community of
Christians needed just for the care of such persons?

If you have considered the doctrine of original sin recently,
these persons will reemphasize your thought. If not, the idea
of original sin will come to you. You will ask: Even in Christian redemption, do the perduring effects of sin continue in
this way? These persons rattle every theological bone in your
body! But then, you should expect this as a faithful pastor.

We come to the end of this book. Each of the chapters
tends to present critical issues of the way of life not only in
the individuals and families who present these problems but
also the way of life of the community as a whole. Your pastoral counseling task is a micro-lab of the larger community.
Personality growth and change call for social growth and
change as well. Your task as an accurately empathic pastor
makes straight your pathway to your work as a prophet for a
whole people in community with one another.

Isaiah 49:8–11: "Thus says the Lord: 'In a time of favor I
have answered you, in a day of salvation I have helped you;
I have kept you and given you as a covenant to the people,
to establish the land, to apportion the desolate heritages;
saying to the prisoners, Come forth, to those who are in
darkness, Appear. They shall feed along the ways, on all bare
heights shall be their pasture; they shall not hunger or thirst,

neither scorching wind nor sun shall smite them, for he who
has pity on them will lead them, and by springs of water will
guide them. And I will make all my mountains a way, and my
highways shall be raised up.' "

SUGGESTIONS FOR FURTHER READING

Cleckley, H. M. *The Mask of Sanity.* 4th ed. C. V. Mosby, 1964.
Hoffman, John C. *Ethical Confrontation in Counseling.* University
of Chicago Press, 1979.
Oates, Wayne E. *Pastoral Counseling.* Westminster Press, 1974.
Schwartz, Richard A., and Schwartz, Ilze K. "Are Personality Dis-
orders Diseases?" *Diseases of the Nervous System,* Vol. 37, No.
11 (November 1976), pp. 613–617.
Scott, P. D. "Symposium on Social Offenders: The Psychopathic
Patient in General Practice." *The Practitioner,* Vol. 218, No.
1308 (June 1977), pp. 801–804.
Virkkunen, Matti. "Self-Mutilation in Antisocial Personality (Dis-
order)." *Acta Psychiatrica Scandinavia,* Vol. 54, No. 5 (Novem-
ber 1976), pp. 347–352.
Woodside, Moya; Harrow, Alan; Basson, John V.; and Affleck,
James W., "Experiment in Managing Sociopathic Behaviour
Disorders." *British Medical Journal,* Vol. 2, No. 6043 (October
30, 1976), pp. 1056–1059.